The
Fowler Family

Early California Pioneers

Eric Storm

GOOD WEATHER PRESS

The Fowler Family: Early California Pioneers
Copyright © 2021 by Eric Storm

First published in 2021.
ISBN: 978-0-578-97801-7 (Paperback)

Good Weather Press
P.O. Box 534
Petaluma, CA 94953

Contents

Guides to the Fowler Family

Fowler Family Tree

William Kitty

Bill Catherine Henry Ann Minerva

© 2020 Eric Storm

Fowler Family Timeline

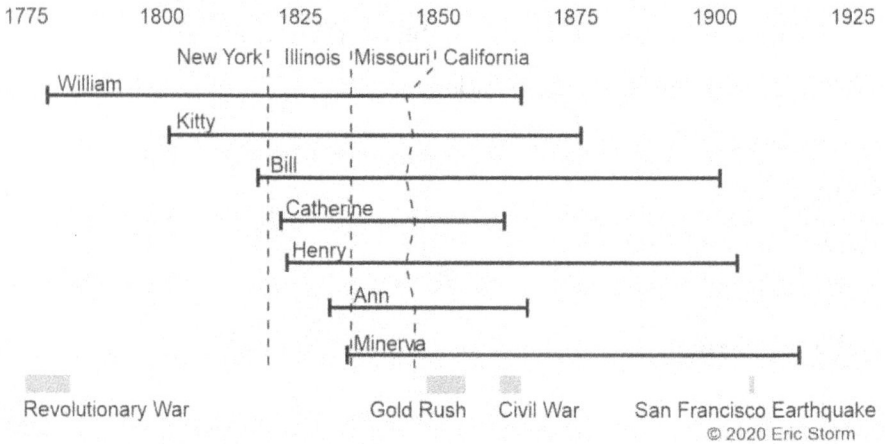

1775   1800   1825   1850   1875   1900   1925

New York Illinois Missouri California

William

Kitty

Bill

Catherine

Henry

Ann

Minerva

Revolutionary War   Gold Rush   Civil War   San Francisco Earthquake

© 2020 Eric Storm

Map of Northern California in the 1840s

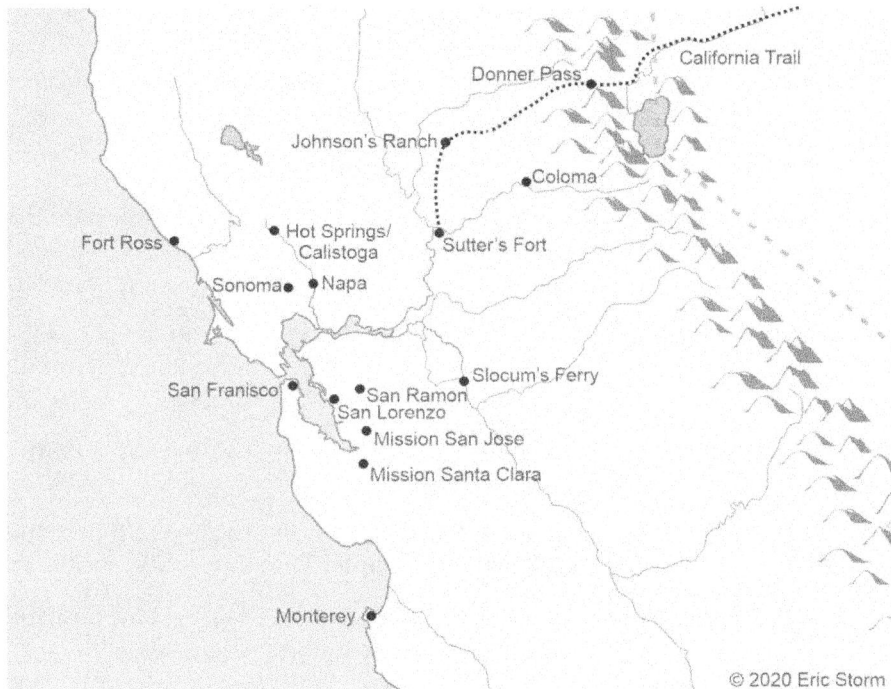

Donner Pass

California Trail

Johnson's Ranch

Coloma

Fort Ross

Hot Springs/
Calistoga

Sutter's Fort

Sonoma • Napa

Slocum's Ferry

San Franisco

San Ramon
San Lorenzo

Mission San Jose

Mission Santa Clara

Monterey

© 2020 Eric Storm

Key People in the Fowler Story

Alfred Musgrave	traveled to California with his brother, Calvin Musgrave
Bidwell-Bartleson Party	first overland group of people on the California Trail, which Bill Fowler joined in 1841
Calvin Musgrave	second husband of Kitty Speed Fowler and father of James Musgrave
Catherine Magness	wife of Henry Fowler
Donner Party	overland group to California that followed the Fowlers and Harlans on the Hastings Cutoff and was trapped in the Sierra during winter of 1846
Dr. Edward Bale	original land grant recipient in Upper Napa Valley where he built a sawmill and gristmill; later sold his land to the Fowlers
Fowler Mallett	grandson of Henry Fowler who wrote a Fowler family history
George Harlan	led Harlan Party to California; second husband of Catherine Fowler Hargrave
George Washington Harlan	cousin of Jacob and Joel Harlan and husband of his first cousin Sarah Harlan
George Yount	first settler in the Napa Valley
Jacob Harlan	traveled to California with his uncle George Harlan and married Ann Fowler
James Musgrave	son of Calvin Musgrave and Kitty Speed Musgrave; born with achondroplasia
Joel Harlan	traveled to California with his father, George Harlan, and married Minerva Fowler
John Fowler Jr.	brother of William Fowler
John Fowler Sr.	immigrated from Scotland to Albany, NY; the father of William Fowler and John Fowler Jr.
John Fremont	U.S. military leader who took part in the U.S. takeover of California
John Hargrave	cousin of William Hargrave and first husband of Catherine Fowler; died on the California Trail

John Sutter	built Sutter's Fort, the initial landing spot and supply station for American immigrants
Kelsey Family	early pioneer family in California and Oregon who traveled and worked with the Fowlers
	David Kelsey – patriarch of the family
	Rebecca Kelsey – first wife of Bill Fowler
	Andrew, Sam, and their brother Ben Kelsey and his wife Nancy – had various encounters with Native Americans
Lansford Hastings	wrote a guide for emigrants suggesting the dangerous Hastings Cutoff
Lewis Musgrave	third husband of Catherine Fowler Harlan; became an outlaw
Lilburn Boggs	ex-governor of Missouri who traveled overland with the Fowlers and whose son, William Boggs, was a friend of Henry Fowler
Malinda Harlan	second wife of Bill Fowler who divorced Bill after four years
Mariano Vallejo	Californio and major land-owner north of San Francisco Bay who hired the Fowlers as carpenters to work on many of his buildings
Peter Storm	early Napa Valley resident who worked for the Fowlers and designed the first flag of the Bear Flag Revolt
Peter Wimmer	brother-in-law to George Harlan who worked on Sutter's Mill with his wife, Jennie Wimmer, and who was present when James Marshall discovered gold
Samuel Brannan	entrepreneur who bought land from the Fowlers and built a hot springs resort at Calistoga
William Hargrave	family friend of the Fowlers, Henry Fowler's business partner, and cousin of John Hargrave
William Winter	traveled with the Fowlers to Oregon and California; traveled with Bill Fowler back to Missouri

Introduction

———— • ————

The history of early California is often told through an accounting of important events and famous people. The Gold Rush, Spanish missions, the Bear Flag Revolt, and the Donner Party are common markers evoking the story of California during the mid-1800s, and names such as Captain John Fremont, General Mariano Vallejo, Sam Brannan, and John Sutter are synonymous with that time.

This is the story of a family who is not well known to history, but their lives offer a window into pioneer life in California during the 1840s. William Henry Fowler, his wife Catherine "Kitty" Speed Fowler, and their five children were among the first to make the arduous and uncertain trip from the Eastern United States to the Pacific Coast. They came from modest roots in New York State, and throughout their lives, they took part in American westward expansion and the transformation of California from Mexican ranchos into Victorian cities. They lived in cabins, cooked over open fires, saw the enormous herds of buffalo on the Plains, and interacted with Native Americans. They found gold, were part of the early development of San Francisco, and eventually owned large tracts of land in the Napa Valley. The Fowlers were a close-knit, hard-working family, and they endeavored to make something of themselves and contribute to the community around them. While their reputations never extended much beyond where they lived, they were, in many respects, more successful than most immigrants to California.

I came across the Fowlers while researching the genealogy of my family. Two branches of my family tree came to California before the Gold Rush: the Carrigers on my mother's side and the Fowlers on my father's. The Carrigers arrived in California in 1846, and Christian Carriger and his wife, Levisa, are my maternal fourth great-grandparents. Their sons Nicholas and Caleb went on to become prosperous farmers in the town of Sonoma.[1] The Fowlers came to Napa Valley in 1844 and 1846, and William and Kitty Fowler are my paternal fourth great-grandparents. Their daughter Catherine Fowler is my third great-grandmother through her daughter, Ella Musgrave.

What started as a genealogy project eventually evolved into an exploration of California's history. Even though the Carrigers have an interesting history of their own, I thought the Fowler family better illustrated the arc of early California pioneers. The Fowlers arrived in the state earlier than the Carrigers, and they experienced what it was like to live as foreigners in Mexican Alta California. They were also more connected to key events such as the Bear Flag Revolt, the development of San Francisco, the Gold Rush, and the Donner Party, and so their tale paints a more comprehensive picture of California in the mid-1800s.

A more holistic accounting of early California considers the pioneers, settlers, and missionaries to be part of an expansionist colonizing force of Euro-Americans that devastated local indigenous people and their culture. Unfortunately, there are few written first-hand accounts from the perspective of Native Americans of this experience. The few that do exist, along with other records, leave no doubt of the abuses and losses indigenous people suffered. I use terms like pioneer, settler, immigrant, and frontier with full acknowledgment of the fact that they were also invaders into the homelands of Native Americans. The Fowlers, like most Euro-Americans who came to California, benefited materially from the colonization carried out by the Spanish and Mexicans who came before them. The Fowlers could "buy" land and "employ" local tribe members because the Native American way of life had been significantly dismantled and was eventually destroyed by Euro-American settlement.

Since the Fowlers were never central to major historical events, information about them is only found as brief mentions in books and documents. There are a few first-hand accounts, diaries, and reminiscences that give specific details about their experiences. Nevertheless, for most of their lives, the details have not been documented, and I could only infer from other events and circumstances at the time. By sifting out the brief references to them and examining the historical context of their world, I have been able to construct some of the narratives of their lives on the frontier. As with many historical accounts, different sources do not always agree. I have used endnotes for additional information along with a selected bibliography to minimize interruptions to the flow of the story and to strike a balance between a readable history and a resource for future researchers. Just as this work benefited from the labors of many other researchers and writers, I hope that my efforts may contribute to future historical and genealogical explorations.

Finally, the family trees of people who lived in small, isolated communities are often complex, as individuals sometimes married multiple times and members of one family often married into the same neighboring family again and again. This is most certainly true of the Fowlers. To help clarify the myriad of relationships, at the end of the book there are family trees of the Fowlers, Musgraves, and Harlans to show the relationships between people as well as note their basic genealogical details.

1

From the Old Country to a New Country

A family's history begins with the oldest known fact or anecdote. In this way, the Fowler family's story starts with John Frederick Fowler, who was born in Scotland in 1740. Who John's parents were and where they lived is unrecorded, and there is no description of his early years.

During the mid-1700s, Scotland was undergoing significant changes that would have far-reaching impacts. The population was growing, resulting in more competition for land. Younger sons had few opportunities if they did not inherit the family farm. New laws weakened the Highland clan system, which had connected clansmen and tribal chieftains to certain areas for centuries. Consequently, many men who would normally be responsible for managing property were left with few options for work in their communities. Alongside these developments were agricultural innovations that changed land uses and ushered in higher rents. With increasingly poor prospects at home, many young Scots felt compelled to immigrate during the mid-1700s to the British Colonies in hopes of finding work and one day owning property.

In the early 1760s, John Fowler likely joined this migration as a young man in his twenties and set out to make a new life for himself in the colonies in the Americas.[2] During this time of peak Scottish immigration, the Hudson River Valley, which runs north to south down the eastern edge of New York State, became the destination for many immigrating Highlanders. The town of Albany was located on the Hudson River and was considered the western edge of the British Colonies at the time. It was common for Scottish immigrants to move to this backcountry since much of the coastal land was already occupied by earlier settlers. What they found was a sparse outpost with an even more extreme climate than Scotland, given Albany's frigid winters and warm muggy summers.

The city of Albany started in the early 1600s as the small village of Beverwijck, which meant "beaver district." As the name suggests, it was a center for fur trading. This was the first Dutch settlement in North America. Established about the same time as Jamestown in Virginia, it holds the distinction of being one of the oldest cities in the United States. Beverwijck was located on the Hudson River, 140 miles upstream from the Dutch colony of New Netherland on the south tip of Manhattan Island, which later became New York City. In the late 1600s, the region around Beverwijck came under British control, and the town was given the name Albany. The area continued to be fought over by the British, Dutch, and French, which suppressed the town's growth for the next hundred years.

In Albany, probably sometime in the 1770s, John Fowler married Ann Eliza Keith. Little is known of Ann's background, except that she was from somewhere in New York State and that she was most likely Scottish, as Keith is a Scottish family name. It would also make sense John would marry someone with Scottish heritage since people typically met and married those with whom they shared a common culture and language.

The American Revolutionary War broke out in 1775 when the Thirteen American Colonies declared their independence from Great Britain. The fighting began in the coastal towns of New England, later moving into Quebec and upper New York State. By 1776, the war had spread to New York Harbor, Virginia, and the Carolinas. Finally, in 1777, the war reached Albany and John and Ann Fowler directly. Ten years earlier, during the French Indian War, the residents of Albany had been forced to offer quarters to British soldiers in their homes, causing considerable resentment among the residents of the town. Consequently, many people living in Albany in 1777 were predisposed to fight against the British when the war arrived.

All men ages 15 to 55 were required to enroll in a local militia, and John Fowler, then around 37 years old, became a private in the 12th Albany County Militia Regiment.[3] His service in the militia was for just three months, from July to October of 1777. During his service, the regiment was involved in the Saratoga Campaign, an important American victory over the British and a turning point in the Revolutionary War. The Revolutionaries outnumbered the British troops, who were undersupplied and deserting. As a result, six times as many British men died in the short bursts of intense fighting. John's regiment was brought in as reinforcements to force the British into retreat and eventual surrender.

In 1779, the Revolutionary War was still being fought, though most of the battles took place in states far from Albany. It is into this world that John and Ann's first son, William Henry Fowler, was born in 1779. Three years later in 1782, just as the war was ending, William's younger brother, John Frederick Fowler Jr., was born.

Unfortunately, John Fowler Sr. did not live to see his sons grow up. On May 1, 1785, at the age of 45, he died in what is now Syracuse, New York. Given John's relatively young age and the fact that he died in a remote area, it seems likely that he passed away from an illness or an accident. This region, located 145 miles west of Albany, was out beyond the edge of American settlements at the time. After the Revolutionary War, this part of

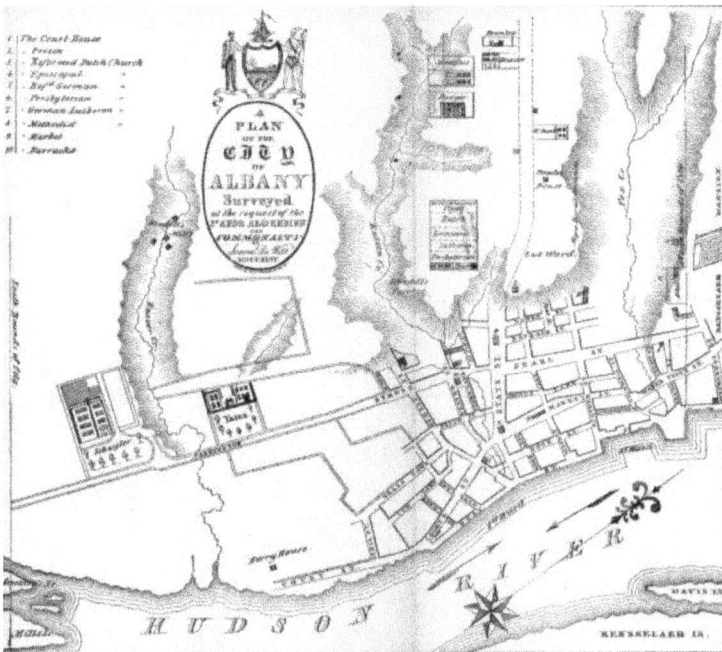

Map of Albany City in 1790

Central New York would become colonized, but, in 1785, it was still the land of the Five Nations of the Iroquois Confederacy. Most of the early travelers who headed to this area went to trade with the people of the Onondaga Nation. From this, it seems likely that John Fowler was a trapper, hunter, or trader on the frontier. Given his original choice to settle in Albany and his later sojourns further west, it may have been that John was drawn to the opportunities of life on the frontier. If this is so, it is a trait that his oldest son, William, would inherit, and which William would pass along as well. In all, four generations of Fowlers, destined by either predilection or circumstance or both, would seek out their fortunes on the edge of this new country.

As a result of John Fowler Sr.'s death, Ann Keith Fowler was widowed with two young children: William, 6 years old, and John, 1 year old. No record of Ann remarrying exists, though this is likely, given that at the time a woman had no legal standing on her own and few options for earning money. At 41 years of age, Ann probably moved in with someone from her own family, and at some point, she may have remarried.

After the Revolutionary War, Albany attracted immigrants and began to grow quickly, and by 1790, it had a population of about 3,500. During this

Albany in the Early 1800s

time, George Washington was the first President of the United States, and the young American republic was testing out its newly found form as a self-governing representative democracy. In 1797, Albany became the capital of New York State, and the increasingly bustling town sprouted breweries, a library, banks, and various churches. As young boys, William and John Fowler grew up in what was a prosperous and quickly changing city.

Running Albany's main printing and publishing company were twin brothers George and Charles Webster. Besides their newspaper and books, they also distributed many copies of their second cousin Noah Webster's Blue Backed Speller. Whether they attended a public school or were home-schooled, William and John Fowler probably learned spelling and grammar from this book which circulated widely at the time.

William Fowler was just 6 years old when his father died, which raises the question of who was in his life to help him learn a trade. John Fowler Sr. may have emigrated from Scotland with a brother named Peter who was a carpenter. There was a Peter Fowler who built the 1815 German Lutheran church in Johnstown, about forty-five miles up the Mohawk Valley from Albany.[4] A young William may have apprenticed with this uncle. However William found his way, over time he became quite skilled as a carpenter and joiner, a trade he would practice his entire life.

As a young man, William Fowler may have had a first wife, though little is known about her. Fowler Mallett, a great-grandson of William, wrote in a family history that William's first wife was of poor health and died when William was in his thirties. It is also unknown if they had children, but it seems unlikely.[5] Later in life, William was devoted to his children, and it would have been out of character for him to have ever abandoned any of them.

According to Mallett's account, William Fowler and his first wife took in an orphaned young woman, Catherine Speed, known to the family as Kitty. Catherine "Kitty" Speed was born on September 24, 1801, in Albany, New York.

Mallett's version of Kitty's childhood is that she was orphaned by Dutch parents who came to Albany via Pennsylvania. After her parents died, the young Kitty was in the care of her uncle, who presumed Kitty was destined to toil in a life of menial labor. When William Fowler was doing some carpentry work for Kitty's uncle, he became aware of her plight. With the uncle's permission, William and his wife took Kitty into their home and

William Henry Fowler

raised her as their daughter. When Mrs. Fowler was in poor health, Kitty took care of her until Mrs. Fowler passed away some time before 1816.[6]

Mallet never says where he got this information, so presumably, it was the family story. His version does a good job of explaining the twenty-year age difference between William and Kitty and the amicable relationship which they maintained their whole lives. There may be other explanations for how William and Kitty got together, but, while Mallett tends to cast family stories in a favorable light, there appears to be no information contradicting this version of events.

What is known is that William and Kitty married in 1816, when she was just 15 and he was about 37. The next year, they had their first child, William Henry Fowler Jr., who was born in September of 1817 and was known in the family as Bill.

By 1810, the population of Albany had tripled in just twenty years to over 10,600 people. It was the tenth-largest city in the nation, and second only to New York City in what was then the most populous state in the country. Roads between towns were being built at a furious pace, and in 1817, construction began on the Erie Canal connecting Albany to Lake

Kitty Speed Fowler

Erie, a project that would transform the state capital into a major transportation hub. Once a settlement on the frontier, Albany had become a
major American city.

The American frontier has always been more of a concept than a fixed
place, describing the open territory just beyond the edge of Euro-American
communities. As new settlements were established, the frontier would be
redefined, usually to the west. For Europeans during the colonial period, the
original thirteen British Colonies were the frontier. They saw these colonies
as wild, faraway places. With the growth of the colonial settlements along
the East Coast, the frontier moved inland about 150 miles up into the
mountains and river valleys. Fur trappers and hunters were often the first
non-indigenous people to venture into this frontier. The relationships they
formed with Native Americans helped the Euro-Americans learn important
land and river routes and the location of good hunting grounds, fertile
valleys, and other resources. For the newly formed United States, places like
Albany had marked the first phase of the frontier, but, over time, these
places were incorporated into the area of established settlements farther
inland from the coast.

There was a pattern to the movement of the frontier which repeated again and again as it shifted westward. First, scouts and map-makers would set out to explore for natural resources, identifying new routes to promising places. Following these trailblazers were the frontiersmen who would move into these newly explored lands and use their backwoods skills to live off the land, often hunting, trapping, and trading furs. Next, guides who had learned the new routes would lead early pioneers who would build cabins and clear forests for farmland. It is at this stage that Euro-Americans often came into conflict with Native Americans and forced them off their home-lands. As more pioneers arrived, they would cluster into budding towns, often little more than a few families living on a well-traveled route. Eventually, these town fathers would set up stores, mills, and other businesses to serve the area. Finally, with enough infrastructure in place, enterprising townsfolk from back East would move in, bringing with them yet more services and institutions like banks, schools, hotels, churches, and other features of Western civilization. Each phase of the opening of the frontier would draw in different people, as well as signal to others that it was time for them to move on.

When the Revolutionary War ended, the 1783 Treaty of Paris esta-blished the western border of the United States at the Mississippi River. Previously, the British had issued the Royal Proclamation of 1763 to slow settlement west of the Appalachian Mountains and to protect Native American lands located there. Those restrictions were removed with the 1783 Treaty, and settlement surged westward from the Appalachians. Stories of backwoodsmen like Daniel Boone filled the American imag-ination with romantic and adventurous fantasies about frontier life. The paths leading west were gradually widened into roads connecting the coastal areas with the interior, as Kentucky, Tennessee, and Ohio became states.

In 1803, the Louisiana Purchase opened up the middle of the continent to even more exploration. A few years later, Lewis and Clark's expedition returned from their two-and-a-half-year journey to the Pacific Northwest with maps and descriptions of the land between the Mississippi and the West Coast. By 1810, the Mississippi River was the leading edge of what was to become the second phase of the western expansion, with St. Louis as the main city and gateway to the West. The former frontier lands between the Mississippi and the Eastern States filled in, as cities and towns sprang up along the newly expanding roads.

By 1817, William and his younger brother John moved out of Albany. Both were married family men by that time. John Fowler married Elizabeth Howey in about 1815, and they soon had their first child.[7] John and his young family headed off to Granville, Ohio, a growing town where he and Elizabeth raised five more children.[8]

There is no record of William and John's mother, Ann Keith Fowler, living with either son as they moved west. This may be further evidence that she eventually remarried. In fact, the only other thing known about Ann Fowler is that she died in 1832.

As for William, it was said that he was a restless soul and that he had a love of the sparsely populated frontier, preferring to have many miles between him and his nearest neighbor. Like many hopeful pioneers, William believed that by moving to a new spot he would find the Promised Land he was looking for. This desire may have been inherited from his father, or a preference he developed during his childhood in early Albany. Whatever the reason, as Albany grew, William decided to move his family out to the frontier for the first, but certainly not the last, time.

2

A Growing Family Moves West

———•———

W ithin months of their son Bill's birth in 1817, William and Kitty
Fowler moved to the Illinois Territory.[9] This was a move of more
than a thousand miles from their home in Albany, New York. Before the
Erie Canal was built, this long journey was most likely made by traveling

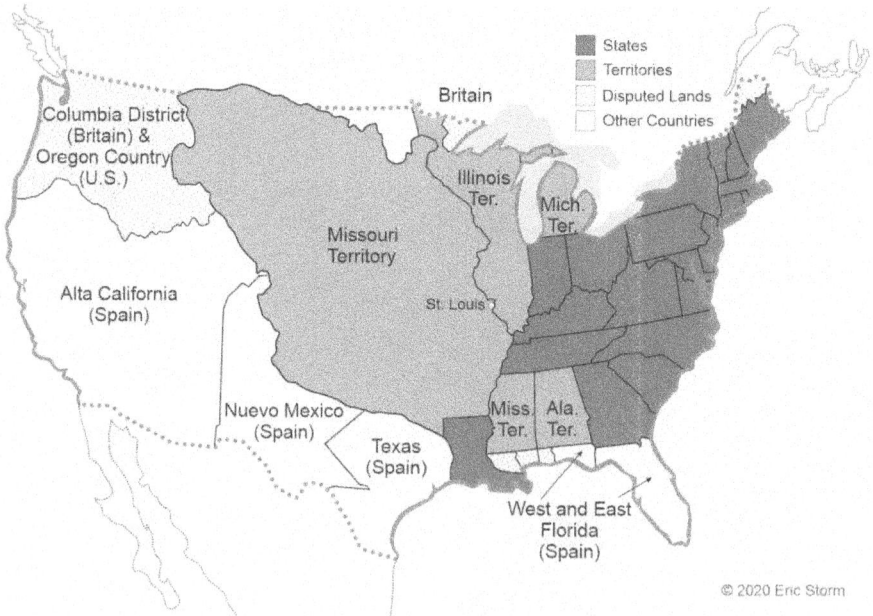

Map of the United States in 1817

overland to Lake Erie, and then by boat down the Ohio River to the Mississippi. The Fowlers settled near the new town of Belleville in southern Illinois Territory, just across the Mississippi River from St. Louis. At the time, St. Louis was the center of government for the newly dubbed Missouri Territory, which stretched west to the Continental Divide. Belleville was in the very early stages of its development, having just been named in 1814 and incorporated as a village not long after the Fowlers arrived. Soon afterward, Illinois became a state at the end of 1818.

Why the Fowlers chose Belleville is not known, though it was one of the many places on the frontier recently open for settlement. They may have also been seeking somewhat better weather, with less extreme winters and longer, though humid, summers. Over the next fifteen years, the Fowlers made their home three miles south of Belleville where they raised five children. Their second child, Catherine Fowler, was born on March 15, 1821. (From here on the name "Kitty" is used to refer to the mother, Catherine Speed Fowler, and the name "Catherine" for her daughter, to avoid confusion and to reflect how they were known in the family.[10]) William and Kitty's third child, John Henry Fowler, was born June 17, 1822, and went by his middle name, Henry. Ann Eliza Fowler was born eight years later on July 4, 1830. Their youngest child was Minerva Jane Fowler, born March 3, 1833. Each of William and Kitty's children would lead very different lives on the American frontier.

Given the eight-year gap between when Henry and Ann were born, it is likely that Kitty lost at least one child during that time. Pregnancy and childbirth were risky in the early 1800s, and even more precarious out on the frontier. Moreover, at the time there was about a one in three chance of a child dying before the age of three. Although miscarriages and early childhood deaths were not always noted in family histories, then as now, the impact on the family, particularly the mother, was often significant.

The Fowlers were one of a handful of families to settle near Belleville, Illinois. In 1825, William opened the area's first coal mine on their property. The coal industry continued to grow in the region, and in 1837, a railroad was built connecting Belleville to St. Louis and Pittsburgh. The development of this important industry and the increased transportation options significantly added to the prosperity of the area.

William also made good use of his carpentry skills, and he was hired to oversee the building of a courthouse in Belleville after the previous one

was deemed too small. He
did the woodwork for the
new brick courthouse that was
completed in June of 1831,
for which he was paid about
$3,000.

Carpentry in the early
1800s was still an artisan
craft with apprenticeships of
four to seven years to
become a journeyman. A
master craftsman would teach
and supervise each stage of a
journeyman's education, including the use of hand tools
to do everything from fram-
ing buildings to constructing
windows, doors, and stairs.
The journeyman carpenter
would then be available for
hire. It would take several

1800 Woodworking Tools

more years until the journeyman could become a master craftsman
himself. William eventually became a master craftsman, and he went on to
teach his sons, Bill and Henry, when they were old enough to become
apprentices.

During this time, carpentry tools were going through a revolution,
though, out on the frontier, William Fowler may have missed out on these
innovations. Many of William's tools were likely hand-made and not the
newer tools made from steel with improved designs. He probably made
frequent use of wooden pegs for joining wood, as nails were hand-forged
and time-intensive, and the newer cut nails were not often found in the
backcountry. He would have had a variety of implements such as an axe,
adz, mallet, saw, plane, hand drill, chisel, and caliper. These tools would
have been precious belongings, which William brought with him as he
moved west. William also designed buildings during his career, and he
accumulated a library of books and papers on architecture which he kept
over his lifetime as well.

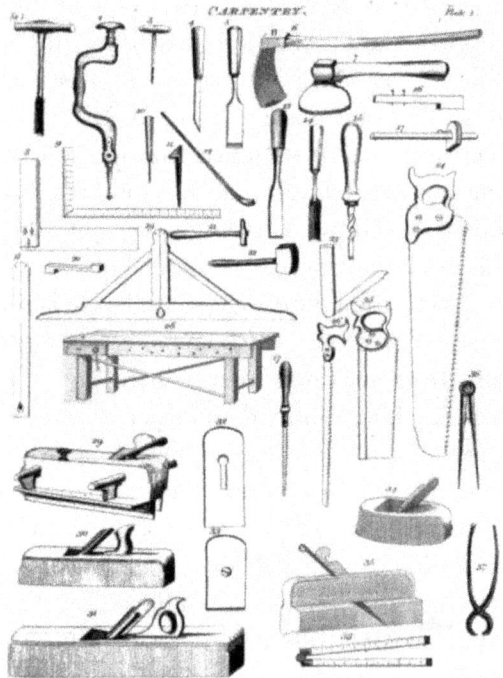

William Fowler stood an imposing six feet tall. While he was often described by others as stern, he was devoted to his friends and family all of his life. He had a reputation for honesty and was considered to be a principled and hard-working craftsman, characteristics that served him well on the frontier.

While William was busy with his carpentry trade and coal mine, which offered some financial stability to an otherwise precarious life, Kitty spent most of her time at home with five children and the chores of a frontier household. Food preservation and preparation would have taken much of Kitty's time. As the children got older, they were able to help with chores such as hauling water, feeding livestock, collecting eggs, milking cows, and churning butter. Cooking would have been done over an open fire in a fireplace, using cast iron pots, frying pans, and Dutch ovens. The latter was particularly ingenious and versatile, and it could be used to bake bread, stew or roast meat, and boil liquids. Laundry took all day and was traditionally done on Mondays, with ironing and mending done on Tuesdays.

Kitty was known for her musical abilities, and she played the violin. She enjoyed singing and belonged to church choirs, which would have likely come as a much-appreciated break from chores. She also taught her children to play the violin, and her daughters became so skillful that they received favorable comments from those who heard them. It is unknown where Kitty acquired these skills, perhaps from William's first wife, or perhaps during her many years in Belleville. In any event, music probably added a welcomed liveliness to pioneer life.

In the 1830s, Belleville began experiencing a large wave of immigration, largely from Germany, bringing money and energy after many years of economic stagnation. These factors, along with Belleville's growth, which paradoxically William had contributed to over the years, may have triggered his desire to seek out the new frontier once more. Whatever comforts and stability the Fowlers had built up over the last fifteen years in Belleville, they were willing to give them up for the opportunity to move west yet again.

In 1833, the Fowler family moved two hundred miles west of Belleville to a spot south of the Osage River, in what was later known as Polk Township, St. Clair County, Missouri.[11] The area was just beginning to be settled by Euro-Americans at that time, and log cabins, hunting, and hard work were the norm. It would be years before the newly forming towns would have schools and churches. The Fowler family was among the earliest settlers to the area, once again choosing to live on the frontier.

At the time of this move, William was 54 years old, Kitty was 32, and their five children ranged in ages from 16 to less than one year old.

Their oldest son, Bill, was a good-looking young man, charming and well-liked. He was also considered a difficult child for his parents, acting recklessly at times. Bill was sent off to study at West Point in New York, although later in life his father, William, felt they were mistaken in choosing to send Bill away.[12] William thought it would have been better to have kept his son close to home where he could provide more oversight and help Bill to temper his restlessness. As it was, once Bill left home, he lived a very adventurous life as a young man, never wanting to stay in one place for long.

In December of 1836, William and Kitty's oldest daughter, Catherine, married John Hargrave. She was just 15 years old. John Hargrave was 17 years old and also came from a Missouri pioneer family.[13] Catherine and John had their first child the following year.

William and Kitty's youngest son, Henry, was 11 years old when the family relocated, and he was probably already beginning to learn his father's carpentry trade. He seemed destined to follow in his father's footsteps as a carpenter, and he only had what little schooling was available on the frontier. Henry and his younger sisters likely learned the basics of reading, writing, and math from their mother and perhaps a local educated person offering lessons.

It is not known exactly what happened or exactly when, but, by about 1840, after twenty-four years of marriage to William Fowler, Kitty married Calvin James Musgrave. It is assumed that Kitty divorced William, though there is no record of it. William did not remarry, and he stayed close to his family. William and Kitty continued to live near one another, amicably sharing Sunday dinners for years, so it seems they parted on good terms. One reason for their separation may have been their age difference; William was 61 and Kitty was 39 when she remarried. In describing this big change, Fowler Mallett noted that their initial relationship was more like a father to a daughter when the Fowlers took Kitty into their home.

Kitty's new husband, Calvin Musgrave, was born in Tennessee and was a descendant of John "The Quaker" Musgrave. John the Quaker and his wife Mary came to the British Colonies in 1682. Five generations later, via North Carolina and Tennessee, Calvin was living in the Missouri Territory where he met Kitty.[14]

While William Fowler was about twenty years older than Kitty, Calvin Musgrave was almost twenty years her junior, younger even than Kitty's oldest son Bill. Significant age differences between husbands and wives were certainly not uncommon at that time, especially on the frontier where there were few eligible women. However, the divorce and remarriage, not to mention the considerable age difference with Kitty's new husband, would have felt like a substantial change in the family nonetheless. In spite of all of this, Calvin was well-liked and respected by Kitty's family. With Calvin, Kitty gave birth to twins in 1841. The boy, James Calvin Musgrave, was born with a medical condition known as achondroplasia, which is the most common cause of dwarfism. Sadly, the girl died in infancy. William and Kitty's youngest daughter, Minerva, was just 6 years old at the time, and so Kitty's new life meant a continuation of her role as wife and a mother of young children on the frontier.

3

On the Oregon Trail

————————————— • —————————————

In his early twenties, Bill Fowler returned to Missouri from his schooling at West Point and studying law. Despite his exceptional education and being admitted to the bar in Illinois, Bill had no desire to settle down and practice law. Instead, he seemed to be drawn to remote areas like his father and grandfather. It did not take long for Bill to make the decision to go west, and in May of 1841, he joined the first emigrant party on the Oregon Trail.[15] While individuals and small groups of trappers, missionaries, and military personnel had previously crossed overland to the Pacific, the Bidwell-Bartleson Party was notable as the first large party made up explicitly of emigrants—individuals and families going with the specific purpose of settling a new territory.

The specific destinations that captured the imaginations of people heading west were Oregon and California. The lands beyond the Great Plains were largely mountainous and arid, and they were still the realm of Native Americans in 1840. However, the small European settlements located along the Pacific Coast were attractive to pioneers looking for land and opportunities. When they talked of going to Oregon, they meant the Hudson Bay Company settlements along the Columbia and Willamette Rivers. Likewise, when people spoke of going to California, they were referring to the Mexican settlements strung along the coastal valleys from San Diego to the San Francisco Bay.

This large migration of Americans going west marked the beginning of the third phase of the frontier, extending from the Rocky Mountains to the Pacific Ocean. This expansion would be different from the previous two waves in a couple of ways. Whereas, before, farmers cleared the land and planted crops, the drier western regions were better suited to cattle ranching and mining. Secondly, the vast expanses of land in the West meant that the pattern of settlement was less dense than in the East, with western towns and cities located farther apart. Ranchers often lived far from town and each other, requiring them to be more self-sufficient. The towns that did exist were often smaller and had fewer services and supplies.

Leading the sixty-person emigrant party bound for California was Captain John Bartleson. The organizer and secretary of the party was 21-year-old John Bidwell. Fortunately, Bidwell kept a diary of his experience, cataloging who was in the group and where and how they traveled. Among those in the Bidwell-Bartleson Party were members of the Kelsey family, whom Bill would have known from Missouri. By chance, the party met up with a group of ten Jesuits who were en route to Oregon. They were led by Pierre-Jean De Smet, a missionary who had lived and worked among the Native Americans, and Thomas "Broken Hand" Fitzpatrick, an experienced mountain man. Their meeting with the Jesuits was fortunate since the Bidwell-Bartleson Party did not include anyone with detailed knowledge of the route. Fitzpatrick was very familiar with the trail and would serve as the guide for both groups. He had traveled and traded in the Rockies for almost twenty years, and he helped popularize the South Pass as the best wagon route over that mountain range.

In spite of their preparations and expertise, the journey was a difficult one. The weather was always a wild card, and the party encountered their share of bad conditions along the way. They also struggled with difficult river crossings. On August 11, 1841, at Soda Springs in present-day Idaho, about half of the people in the Bidwell-Bartleson Party, including Bill Fowler and some of the Kelseys, decided to split off and join the mountain guide Fitzpatrick and the Jesuit missionaries as they headed for Oregon. Despite Fitzpatrick's warnings, the remaining thirty-two people led by Bartleson and Bidwell were determined to reach California. Andrew Kelsey, Benjamin Kelsey, Benjamin's wife Nancy, and their infant daughter were among those who chose to continue as previously planned. With no one to guide them, the group turned southwest to cross the Nevada Desert, a perilous journey they were fortunate to survive. While they would have to abandon their wagons in the eastern Nevada desert, this contingent of the Bidwell-Bartleson Party became the first emigrant party to travel along what would later be known as the California Trail.

On September 24, 1841, a farmer working for a Methodist Mission at The Dalles in Oregon noted in his diary that Bill Fowler and several others had passed by. At that point, Bill and his group were two weeks ahead of the main Jesuit party.[16] The Dalles was a twelve-mile stretch of rapids on the Columbia River before the water cuts through a deep gorge. From The Dalles, Bill Fowler and the others took rafts and floated down the Columbia River, through rapids and over portages, to Fort Vancouver and Oregon City. They were in the vanguard of emigrant parties headed to Oregon, and over the next twenty-five years, 300,000 people would make this same journey.

The Oregon Country was a jointly occupied and disputed territory among the British, French, and Americans. It covered the entire Pacific Northwest, and the conflict over the region was not resolved until 1846. The Oregon Treaty separated the United States from British North America (later to become Canada) at the 49th parallel. The main settlement in Oregon Country was Fort Vancouver, on the northern bank of the Columbia River across from present-day Port-

Map of Oregon Country in 1841

land. The fort was the center of the Hudson Bay Company's fur trading activities in the area, and John McLoughlin was the Chief Factor and Superintendent. He encouraged immigrants to head south to Oregon City, located twenty-five miles along the Willamette River from the Columbia River and Fort Vancouver.

Bill Fowler over-wintered in Oregon City in 1841-1842. It was quickly growing into a town, as new homes, a church, mills, and a store were built. It was a natural site for a settlement, with abundant resources nearby, including water to power mills from the Willamette Falls. Originally, the name for the small community had been Willamette Falls, but it would take on the emblematic designation of Oregon City in 1842.

With the rising population in mind, Superintendent John McLoughlin made plans for the building of a new grist mill in Oregon City. Grist mills were among the first major projects in a community, given the importance of grinding wheat and other grains into flour for food. Bill Fowler offered himself as a candidate for the undertaking. Bill's education and charm were probably in his favor, as was the fact that Bill's father, William Fowler, had experience running large construction projects. In the end, Bill secured a contract with McLoughlin to build the mill and possibly other buildings in the area. To fulfill his promises, Bill needed to bring to Oregon the right expertise, namely his father and members of the Kelsey family who were themselves millwrights.

With a contract in hand, Bill Fowler turned around and did what few others before him had done; he headed back to Missouri, braving the arduous trail once more. In 1842, there were only a couple of parties headed east, and Bill joined one of them. The most plausible is the party that left in June and included the Jesuit, Father De Smet, with whom Bill had traveled on the trail to Oregon just a few months earlier.

When Bill arrived in Missouri in late 1842, having survived the overland route twice, he brought with him the promise of significant work in Oregon City for both his father, William, and his brother, Henry. Despite William being relatively old for such a challenge at age 63, the prospect of an adventure must have appealed to him. He and Henry quickly agreed to follow Bill out to Oregon. Together they set out to assemble an experienced team of builders and millwrights to accompany them.

At the top of the list was David Kelsey. The Kelseys were among the first pioneer families to move to St. Clair County, Missouri in the 1830s.[17]

Map of the Oregon Trail with Depiction of Prairie Schooner

David Kelsey had been a frontiersman, and he and his wife had a family of ten children. Some in the Kelsey family were millwrights, and four of David Kelsey's sons had already traveled west with the Bidwell-Bartleson Party. In 1843, David, his wife, and his younger children made arrangements to head to Oregon with the Fowler men. It was no doubt helpful that William Fowler had worked with the Kelseys on previous projects as well.

Rounding out this team was William Hargrave, a friend of Henry Fowler's and the cousin of John Hargrave, Catherine Fowler Hargrave's husband.[18] Hargrave's decision to join the Fowlers in this endeavor would be the beginning of what would be a lifelong connection to the family.

Given their carpentry skills, it is not surprising that the Fowlers built their own wagon for the trip. While people used all kinds of wagons and carts to make the journey, the Prairie Schooner became the most common type on the Oregon Trail. These wagons were twenty-three feet in length and ten feet tall and were covered with an iconic waterproofed canvas bonnet. The box of the wagon was about four feet wide, ten feet long, and two feet deep, and it was waterproofed so it could be used as a raft during deep water crossings. The iron-banded wooden wheels were of different sizes front and back. The smaller forty-four-inch front wheels allowed for easier turning, while the larger fifty-inch back wheels helped move over rough terrain.

In the spring of 1843, William and his sons, Bill and Henry, set off with their team on the Oregon Trail. Remaining in Missouri were Kitty and Catherine with their new families, and the youngest Fowler girls, Ann and Minerva. The separation from loved ones was significant. Kitty and the Fowler girls probably did not have news of the Fowler men for over two years, though an occasional letter or word may have made its way to them via returning travelers.

The Fowlers, the Kelseys, and William Hargrave were traveling with a party led by Captain John Gantt. It was the largest overland party up until that time, with about 700 people and over 100 wagons. Gantt led the group to Fort Hall on the Snake River in present-day Southeast Idaho. Bill Fowler also served as a guide along the way, drawing on his past overland experiences.

After Fort Hall, previous parties had abandoned their wagons and continued on foot or horseback due to the very rough terrain and the considerable obstacles along the trails. In 1840, a group starting at Fort Hall traveled with three stripped-down wagons and made it to the Columbia River in Oregon, proving that it was conceivable for wagons to make the journey. At last, the Gantt Party with its large number of able-bodied men had the manpower needed to clear the rocks and trees on the trail and make it feasible for loaded wagons. As a result, the Gantt Party became the first wagon train to make it all the way from Missouri to Oregon intact.

Equally important to their success was missionary Marcus Whitman, who helped the pioneers by replenishing their food supplies. The mission he set up was near the Walla Walla River, twenty miles from the Columbia River. Many of those in the party were nearing the end of their provisions, and so the opportunity to restock was critical. The Fowlers were among those grateful for the fresh supplies, and Henry Fowler would speak of his appreciation for Marcus Whitman's foresight for many years.

As the party approached the Deschutes River, they encountered Native Americans from the Walla Walla tribe. Henry Fowler told a version of this story when he was interviewed by historian Hubert Howe Bancroft in 1886.[19]

> *We had no trouble anywhere until we got to the Columbia. ... Before we got to [the Deschutes] river the Indians undertook to rob us. It was generally understood that there was no danger from them, and we had exchanged our guns for the greater necessities and had only two guns left. Two of the men had fallen behind, and they undertook to rob them. We went back to where they were and 60 or 70 Indians came over. We parleyed with them there for a long time. We expected they would shoot us. There seemed to be a chief, a nice looking young man about 28 or 30 years old who was dressed in a nice buckskin suit. We*

were getting ready to start when he came. He wanted us to stop. He said he would make them bring everything back, but we went on and they followed us about 5 miles trying to make us stop, so he told us to camp on the river and he would make them bring everything back. Then they undertook to rob three other men who did not belong to our mess. Then they undertook to rob others that we thought were out of danger and who had all broken up into little squads. They would steal our horses and hide them and bring them back for a shirt. We got tired of that and when they came into camp, Swift and myself had carried our guns, and taking these we told them to go. There we secured our horses, and next morning they came over and robbed two men. The Walla Walla Indians are very mean Indians. They would not interfere with the Hudson Bay men at all. They called us Boston men, and the Hudson Bay men they called King George men. They thought it perfectly right to rob Boston men.

Fort Vancouver

As with all overland journeys, there were hardships, long days, and demanding physical work every step of the way. William Fowler was, and would remain for the rest of his life, one of the oldest men on the frontier. To pick up and head off to parts unknown was ambitious for a man half his age. However, there is no mention of William not being up to the task. In fact, his experience and skills were often highly valued, and his maturity and level-headedness proved beneficial in handling difficult circumstances. In the end, despite the incredible rigors of the journey, all of the Fowlers and the Kelseys arrived safely in Oregon City five months after setting out.[20]

Once again Bill was to spend a gray and wet winter in Oregon City, only this time he had his family and other members of the construction team as company. He had another reason to celebrate as well. On December 12, 1843, Bill, then 26 years old, married Rebecca Kelsey, David Kelsey's 24-year-old daughter. It was just one of many romances that blossomed on the overland trails. A year and a half earlier in June 1841, Rebecca Kelsey's brother Isaiah had married during the journey to Oregon, making him one of the very first to tie the knot on the California and Oregon Trails.[21]

When interviewed in 1886, Henry recalled the grist mill they worked on for McLoughlin, describing the huge timbers they used to frame the two-story building.[22] He said the mill was later washed away during a flood. Several other mills, schools, and churches were built during that time. Oregon City continued to grow at a rapid pace with the arrival of large numbers of immigrants, and there was surely a great demand for experienced carpenters and millwrights.

The Fowlers must have done a good job on the projects they undertook. As a result of their efforts, William Fowler received a letter of recommendation from a Catholic priest stating that he was a good Catholic and carpenter. This letter of recommendation was from Reverend Modeste Demers, the first priest of Oregon City. It was written to Padre Jose Lorenzo de la Conception Quijas of the missions in Sonoma and San Rafael in Alta California. The letter would turn out to be important because it ultimately paved the way for William Fowler to land good work in the Mexican-held territories to the south.

4

From Oregon to California

———— • ————

The newly arrived immigrants in Oregon inevitably debated the pros and cons of the territory as a desirable place to settle. The climate was milder than back East, and there was plenty of land to be claimed. Americans had a growing presence in the region, which was reassuring to some. On the other hand, the persistent rain lasting more than half the year was depressing to some would-be settlers. Also, the labor required to clear the thickly forested land was considerable before any type of settlement or farming was possible. Some disillusioned pioneers regretted their choice to move to Oregon, and they headed south to the warmer and drier climes of Mexican Alta California.

Likewise, immigrants in California also took stock of their choice. Rumors were circulating that Americans were not welcomed by the Mexicans who ruled the territory. Additionally, California was generally more arid and had less land suitable for growing crops, compelling many landowners to take up cattle ranching. Not surprisingly, some immigrants decided to head north to Oregon where the culture was more familiar and the rainfall was abundant, to say the least.

In 1843, one group of pioneers left Oregon and another left California, each heading for the other destination. Lansford Hastings set off from Oregon with fifty men on horseback including Samuel Kelsey, who was one of the Kelsey brothers. Taking off from California was Joel Walker, leading a group of emigrants and bringing with him many head of cattle to sell in Oregon. Members of the Kelsey family who had earlier gone to California with the Bidwell-Bartleson Party, namely Andrew, Benjamin, and Nancy Kelsey, were among those going north with the Walker Party.

Eventually, these two parties met up in the Siskiyou Mountains, near the present-day border of Oregon and California. Upon meeting his north-bound siblings, Samuel turned around and went with them to Oregon City, where the whole Kelsey family was reunited. One can imagine the Kelseys comparing notes about their respective experiences. In the end, they concluded that the weather, the land, and the opportunities for work in California were more appealing. By the spring of 1844, all but a few Kelseys decided to head south.[23]

In June of 1844, William, Henry, and Bill Fowler, along with Bill's new wife, Rebecca Kelsey Fowler, and William Hargrave joined the Kelseys and a few others on the Siskiyou Trail to California. There were thirty-seven people in all, twenty of whom were part of the extensive Kelsey clan, including thirteen women and children. The rest of the party was made up of men from America, England, France, Mexico, and four different Native American tribes. While most were recent immigrants, a few men had been hired from the Hudson Bay Company as guides. This group would become known as the Kelsey Party.[24]

The trip entailed a six-week journey on horseback, down through Oregon's Willamette Valley and over three mountain ranges before heading towards Mount Shasta in California. The steep and thickly forested trail did not allow for wagons, and pack animals were used to carry belongings and supplies.

At the time, travelers on the Siskiyou Trail considered the area danger-ous because of the Native American tribes who lived there. The tribes and travelers often had encounters that led each to become suspicious, fearful, and aggressive toward the other. While some tribes were known to be peaceful and open to trading, others were said to be hostile and prone to ambushing parties to steal goods and animals. When Ben and Nancy Kelsey traveled through the area with Joel Walker the previous year, they clashed with a local tribe, and in retaliation, they mistreated and killed several Native Americans. Joel Walker offered later parties the following advice, shown below as written.[25]

> *Be careful to never camp in the timber if it can be avoided.*
> *Be careful to never Let any Indians come amongst you*
> *Never Lit the Indian have any ammunition on any account*
> *Keep close watch both night and day*

Never neglect camp guard on any account
Never fire a gun after (after) crossing the Umqua mountain untill
    you cross the siskiew mountain perhaps Five days travel
Keep yourselves close as possible in traveling through the Brush
Never scatter after game or [make] any other division
Keep your guns in the best firing condition

The Native Americans of the Umpqua River Valley were not considered a threat, except perhaps to small parties. While the Kelsey Party was in that valley, a French-Native American man from their party brought twenty men from the local tribe into camp to perform a war dance. William Winter, a member of the party, described it at length. He wrote that the men dressed in elk-hide armor hats and vests with their foreheads painted white and that they waved bows and arrows as they danced and sang in a forceful manner. It seemed to have the desired effect of intimidating the pioneers, as Winter wrote their dance "would compel the stoutest nerves to cringe."[26]

The Kelsey Party's fear of attack was particularly keen as they crossed over to the Rogue River Valley in Southern Oregon. The name Rogue River derives from the early characterizations of the local tribes as "rogues" by French fur trappers who had been ambushed in the area. As the Kelsey Party navigated the mountains, guards were positioned on all sides of the group, and some wore extra clothes to protect against arrows. In the end, the group passed into the valley without incident.

Their next encounter occurred after crossing the Rogue River, where thirty local Native Americans came within six hundred feet of the party's camp, apparently to assess if the people trespassing in their territory were friendly or not. After reassurances from the Kelsey Party members, the Native Americans slowly moved closer and sat down sixty feet away. Winter admired the tribe's ability not to show the fear he assumed they also felt. Members of the party prepared a pipe with tobacco and joined the tribe seated in a circle. Together they smoked the pipe as a sign of peaceful intentions on both sides. The Native Americans promised to return the following morning, which they did, bringing beaver skins in trade for various objects the party had.

At the border of Oregon and California, the Kelsey Party made their way over the Siskiyou Mountains, again taking precautions against attack, but passing safely once more. Gradually with each valley, the terrain became drier as they left the forests of Oregon and entered the grasslands of California. The party continued toward Mount Shasta, known then as Snowy Butte, a spectacular snow-capped volcanic peak rising high above the other mountains in a near-perfect cone. They camped for a while below the foot of the mountain at a place Henry Fowler called Soda Springs, probably near present-day Dunsmuir, California. Naturally carbonated mineral water poured out of springs into a small basin. Henry recalled that "the party grew fat on the finest biscuit ever tasted, the dough being both mixed and raised by the use of the carbonated water."[27]

Finally, in July of 1844, the Kelsey Party followed the Sacramento River down into the large grassy expanse of the Sacramento Valley. At Cache Creek in present-day Yolo County, they came across their first house since the Willamette Valley, five hundred miles away. They made camp nearby on land owned by William Gordon, taking time to recuperate and regroup before deciding where to head next.

5

Arriving in Alta California

———— • ————

For the next month, the Fowlers and the Kelsey Party camped at Gordon's Ranch, twenty-five miles from Sutter's Fort. The fort was the main settlement in the area and served as the gateway to California for Americans arriving overland.

John Sutter, the namesake of the fort, was a Swiss-German immigrant who had received a large land grant of almost 49,000 acres near present-day Sacramento in the Central Valley. The Mexican-appointed governor of Alta California tasked Sutter with encouraging newly arrived Americans to settle inland, rather than in the coastal area where most of the Mexican settlements were located. A small town of immigrants formed around the fort, which Sutter named New Helvetia, or "New Switzerland." Sutter was intent on building an agricultural and ranching empire, but he had grown the enterprise so quickly that he was constantly in debt.

During a visit to Sutter's Fort, the Fowlers and the other members of the Kelsey Party applied for naturalization, a requirement of all foreigners immigrating to the Mexican-held territory. Unfortunately, by this time, Bill Fowler's marriage to Rebecca Kelsey was falling apart. Upon arriving at Sutter's Fort, Rebecca left Bill and requested a divorce. To appeal Rebecca's claim for divorce, Bill wrote to Thomas Larkin, who was the American Consul for Alta California in Monterey. Larkin wrote his reply to Bill on Christmas Eve of 1844, in what historian Lin Weber cites as the first known record of marriage counseling in the American West:[28]

Map of the San Francisco Bay Area in 1844

You complain that your wife has left you and refuses any longer to live with you, that she has no cause for leaving that you have ever treated her well, boarded and clothed her in a loving manner, and to the best of your means. In case what you state to be true, your wife has no right to leave you ... But in case your wife will not live with you, it remains for you to point out some respectable house where she shall live. She has no right to go from place to place without your permission. ...

Should there once have been cause on your part to make your wife unhappy I would advise you, as you value your peace of mind, your character, and future wealth and well being, to exert yourself in doing all you can to make your wife's situation with you pleasant and happy. ...

In the mean time do nothing by force or in anger, make no angry remarks respecting your wife, tell no stories true or false against her as all this makes this separation more distant, injures her and redounds not to your credit.

Larkin also wrote to Rebecca:[29]

Your husband say that if you will return and live with him, he promises you and myself, to do his best to make your situation and life a happy one, and that should you hereafter ever have reason to complain of him, you have his full consent to apply to me for advice and assistance. ...

I wish you to inform me why you left your husband, and why you still refuse to live with him. ... I advise you to live with your husband, I also promise to aid and protect you in every possible manner if Mr. Fowler does not take care of you or ill treats you. In the mean time keep a strict care over your own conduct, that you give your husband no just cause or imaging one to complain of you. ...

Wishing that I may be the means of again uniting yourself and husband I am your friend and humble servant.

Despite Bill's plea and Larkin's advice to the couple to try and make amends, Rebecca was granted a divorce.[30]

While Oregon Country was not part of the United States, it was occupied by Americans as well as by other English speakers. The culture, regulations, and language would have been familiar to most Americans arriving in the territory. Alta California, on the other hand, was Spanish-speaking and had developed a distinctive culture during its colonization by Spain and later Mexico. The Fowlers had arrived in a foreign country, one that was undergoing great change.

Mexican-ruled Alta California comprised a vast swath of land from the Rocky Mountains to the Pacific Coast and from the 42nd parallel in the north to San Diego in the south. Since virtually all of the settlement was along the Pacific Coast, the name California was often used to describe an area similar to the boundaries of the present-day state.

California had once been home to one of the largest populations of Native Americans in North America, estimated to have numbered up to

Map of Alta California in 1845

300,000 people. Due to the relatively moderate climate and abundant food sources, hundreds of tribes lived in relative peace along the fertile coasts and valleys. The arrival of Europeans in the late 1700s had a devastating impact on people who had inhabited the region for thousands of years. With the Europeans came diseases, increased violence, and the introduction of non-native plants and land-use practices which led to the decimation of Native American tribes and the destruction of their cultures. By 1845, the Native population was estimated to have declined to 150,000, or possibly as little as 30,000, as a result of the Euro-American takeover of the area.

The arrival of the Europeans in California was the consequence of long-term explorations spreading both east and west around the globe. The Spanish had traveled west and landed in Central America, then colonized the lands up the Pacific coast into North America, eventually reaching the valleys north of the San Francisco Bay. Conversely, the Russians had made their way east across Asia and the Bering Sea, ultimately traveling south along the Pacific coast and establishing Fort Ross with occasional excursions to Bodega Bay and the San Francisco Bay. It was in the area just north of the San Francisco Bay, in present-day Sonoma County, where the Europeans traveling east and west met up on the other side of the globe. These distant explorations strained each country's chains of supplies and command, making California a formidable frontier for all concerned.

In response to Russia's exploration of the Pacific coast, the Spanish built missions from Mexico up into Alta California to stake their claim in this region of the New World. They had not succeeded in persuading settlers to move out to what was seen as a remote wilderness, so the task was left to the Catholic Church. The Franciscan missionaries were sent out to convert the Native Americans to Christianity, though in practice the indigenous people were treated more like slave labor. The Native Americans who entered mission communities were not allowed to come and go freely and suffered from foreign diseases, radical changes in diet and culture, and physical abuse. Over time, the Church found it increasingly difficult to supply and maintain the missions, especially those built farther up the coast from Mexico.

Responsibility for the missions shifted from Spain to a newly independent Mexico in 1821, though the connection remained tenuous between Monterey, the capital of Alta California, and Mexico City, located 1,800 miles to the south. The instability of the new Mexican government, the geographic remoteness of Alta California, and its low population meant the region remained a marginally controlled and far-off frontier.

The Franciscans who founded and ran the missions were Spanish, but after Mexican Independence, they lost their standing and power and most left the region for Spain. The authority shifted to the native-born Californios, who were the children of soldiers, sailors, and convicts and who had lived their entire lives on the frontier of Alta California. Over the years the Californios became a mixture of different races and ethnicities, including Native American and other European nationalities that had arrived in the area and married into Californio families. European-Californio marriages were not uncommon, as it was often the quickest and most sure way for Euro-Americans to become Mexican citizens and thereby eligible to own land.

The economy of Alta California was based on cattle ranching. The drier climate and large ranges of the West were more conducive to grazing animals than tilling soil. Moreover, the Californios seemed to prefer the somewhat more relaxed lifestyle of ranching over the daily toil of farming. The main products from cattle ranching were cowhides and tallow rendered from beef fat. The hides were shipped east where the leather was primarily used for shoemaking and belting in machinery. The tallow was sent to South America to be used in candle and soap manufacturing.[31]

Californio culture was shaped by the circumstances of life on the frontier. Given the relatively weak governmental control in the area, maintaining strong personal and family relationships was paramount. Generous hospitality helped to reinforce these relationships, and it was also important in an area of far-flung settlements and a sparse population. The Californios created many reasons to gather together and celebrate, including weddings, fiestas, and rodeos. These occasions gave the women a chance to dress up and show off their dancing skills and the men an opportunity to demonstrate their fine horsemanship.

Horses were a central feature of Californio life. Visiting foreigners often commented on the highly developed horsemanship of the locals, saying that they did everything on a horse, including going next door. Horses were critical to both the Californios and the Native American *vaqueros* for traveling over long distances and tending livestock. The horses were generally allowed to roam free, only being caught as needed for transportation. A rider might use two or three different horses successively on a long journey. The Californios developed a unique saddle design with a large horn on the front of the saddle, which allowed a rider to secure his lasso and use the horse's weight and maneuverability to subdue cattle, bulls, and even grizzly bears. Riders were also said to be able to pick up items from the ground without dismounting and to relish displaying their equestrian expertise at events like horse races and bullfights.

To reduce the power of the Catholic Church in their affairs, Mexico pushed for the secularization of the missions. This policy further contributed to the end of the mission system throughout Alta California. The Californios took Church-held lands and redistributed them in the form of land grants for cattle ranching. Those Californios with the means or connections were able to secure land, and under this land grant system, wealthy Californios became a sort of landed aristocracy.

By 1836, the sense of frustration among the Californios with the central Mexican government was so strong that they tried staging a revolt. While they were unsuccessful politically, they did gain more autonomous control over the region. The Californios thought of Alta California as their territory more than as a part of Mexico, but their power in the region was neither complete nor secure.

The number of Americans in California had begun to swell in 1841 with the arrival of groups like the Bidwell-Bartleson Party. In contrast, the Russians were leaving the area with the decline in the fur trade. In 1841, they sold their primary outpost at Fort Ross on the north coast to John Sutter. By 1845, about seven hundred American and European immigrants, mostly men, had settled around the San Francisco Bay and near Sutter's Fort in the Central Valley. While Californios numbered around 6,000 at this time, the majority were women and children, and only about 1,500 were adult men. Moreover, most of the Californios lived in the southern parts of Alta California, near present-day San Diego and Los Angeles.

The future of Alta California was uncertain, and opinion was divided about who would ultimately control the territory. The primary contenders were the United States, England, and France. As the French explorer Eugène Duflot de Mofras wrote in the early 1840s:[32]

> California will belong to whatever nation chooses to send
> there a man-of-war and two hundred men. ... since California
> must change masters, we should prefer to see it in the hands
> of the United States rather than in those of England.

Upon arriving in California, William Fowler and his sons, Bill and Henry, went to work right away. In the summer of 1844, they found employment as carpenters at Sutter's Fort. In the fall, they worked in Pope Valley, about fifty miles west of Sutter's Fort and nestled in the Coastal Mountains running between the Central Valley and the Pacific Coast. After Pope Valley, they traveled south twenty-three miles to the small town of Sonoma located just north of San Francisco Bay.

In Sonoma, the Fowlers met General Mariano Vallejo, the Military Commander and Director of Colonization of the Northern Frontier and one of the most powerful men in Alta California. He had a large 66,662-acre rancho, making up the over one hundred square miles of land on which he ran cattle. Vallejo had overseen the decommissioning of the mission in Sonoma in 1833, and he established a small pueblo there where he and his family lived.

The new pueblo of Sonoma had been a military outpost since the secularization of the mission, but it did not have a town council until 1844.

Charles Wilkes, an American naval officer and explorer, visited Sonoma and described the condition of the town in 1841 in his expedition report:[33]

> *Upon paper, Zonoma* [sic] *is a large city, and laid out according to the most approved plan. In reality, however, it consists of only the following buildings: General Vallejo's house, built of adobes, of two stories, which fronts on the public square, and is said to be one of the best houses in California. On the right of this is the residence of the general's brother, Salvadore, and to the left, the barracks for the accommodation of the guard for the general, consisting of about twenty fusiliers* [sic]. *Not far removed is the old dilapidated mission-house of San Francisco Solano, scarcely tenantable, though a small part of it is inhabited by the Padre Kihas* [sic], *who continues, notwithstanding the poverty of his mission, to entertain the stranger, and show him all the hospitality he can.*
>
> *Besides the buildings just enumerated, there were in the course of construction, in 1841, a neat little chapel, and a small building for a billiard-room. There are also three or four more houses and huts which are tenanted; and at some future day it may boast of some farther additions.*

Skilled craftsmen were in short supply in Alta California, and General Vallejo undoubtedly welcomed the arrival of men with experience and education like the Fowlers. Many of the new immigrants brought with them much-needed expertise and knowledge as doctors, engineers, blacksmiths, and carpenters. William Fowler had his letter of recommendation in hand and was probably introduced to Vallejo by Padre Quijas. The Fowler men started working on various building projects for Vallejo, making what was then a good wage of two and a half dollars a day. The Fowlers and William Hargrave spent the winter of 1844 working in Sonoma, acquiring the funds they would need to establish their own homesteads.

6

Putting Down Roots in the Napa Valley

————— • —————

In the fall of 1844, on their way from Pope Valley to Sonoma, the Fowlers would have traveled through Napa Valley for the first time. Like the Sonoma Valley, the Napa Valley is one of the small picturesque valleys that lie north of the San Pablo and San Francisco Bays. The valley is flanked by the Mayacamas Mountains to the north and west, and by the Howell Mountains to the east. The upper end of the valley floor is only a little more than a mile wide, and it is surrounded by forested hills and towering cliffs. Throughout this section of the valley, there are numerous streams, springs, and natural hot springs, as well as the Napa River, which at this point is no more than a creek. The climate is marked by mild, rainy winters and hot, dry summers. Napa Valley was home to numerous indigenous tribes who found the area rich with edible plants and wild game. The native oats naturally grew a few feet high, much to the amazement of the new immigrants. Henry Fowler described Napa Valley as near Paradise.

Many of the earliest pioneers who came through the valley hunted the abundant game animals for food and skins.[34] Deer and elk were numerous, and their meat was considered the best to eat such that no one seemed to bother hunting the large flocks of ducks and geese. Local predators included mountain lions, wolves, black bears, and grizzly bears. Grizzly bears were so numerous as to be a constant problem. People would frequently cross paths with grizzlies, which preyed on livestock, and every family in the Upper Napa Valley had vivid stories of their run-ins with *Ursus arctos horribilis.*

In 1845, William and Henry Fowler decided they would move to the Napa Valley to set up their homestead alongside a small handful of settlers and a few hundred members of the Wappo tribe. Bill Fowler did not go with his father and brother. Instead, he traveled over the Sierra once again to Missouri, this time with the mission of bringing the rest of the Fowler family to California.

At the time, the Napa Valley delineated the northern edge of Euro-American habitation in Alta California, and there were no other settlements between where the Fowler's built their home and the Willamette Valley, 425 miles to the north. Setting up along the edge of the frontier was a choice William probably found quite appealing. While not the first pioneer in the valley, William Fowler at age 66 was the oldest by 15 years.[35]

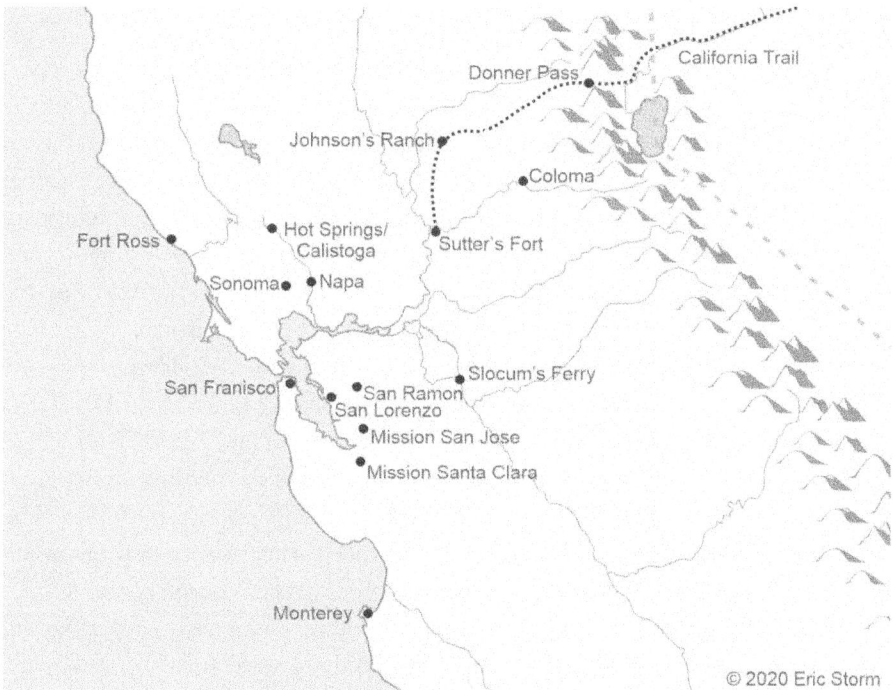

Map of Northern California in 1845

Residents in the Napa Valley at this time included George Yount, who was the original Euro-American settler and landowner in the area, arriving around 1831. He obtained two land grants from the Mexican government in 1836 and 1843 totaling over 16,000 acres. His holdings lay in the middle of the valley, surrounding what is the present-day town of Yountville.

Yount was a hunter and trapper who liked living on the frontier, and he got along well with the local Native Americans. William Fowler probably saw Yount as a man after his own heart. Of all the settlers in the area, Yount and William were the closest in age, though Yount was only 51. Both men had a mature but modest demeanor, not at all interested in attracting too much attention. Moreover, they both worked for Vallejo as carpenters.

Certainly one of the most unique early Euro-American inhabitants in the valley was Peter Storm, a tattooed seaman from Norway. He had come to California in the 1830s and moved to the Napa Valley in 1844. Storm was a craftsman with many talents, some of which would play a key role in the history of California. [Peter Storm is not related to the author.]

Another early settler was Dr. Edward Bale, an English ship's surgeon who had been shipwrecked off Monterey in 1837. He chose to stay in California, serving as a medical doctor around Monterey and the San Francisco Bay Area. He received a land grant in 1841 after marrying Maria Ygnacia Soberanes, General Vallejo's niece. Bale's 18,000-acre land grant included the upper end of the Napa Valley, seven miles up the valley from George Yount. He lived with his family in an adobe, a Spanish-style home made from dried mud bricks. Bale, more than any other landowner, was willing to sell property to Americans, and in this way, he was singularly responsible for the concentration of Americans in the Napa Valley in early California.

Nine miles further up the valley from Dr. Bale's adobe, William and Henry Fowler built a wood cabin for themselves and William Hargrave on Dr. Bale's property. Their new home was next to where Benjamin and Nancy Kelsey had earlier set up a hunting camp. The Fowler's cabin was the first non-indigenous structure built in what would come to be known as the Upper Napa Valley. The cabin once stood on the main route in the valley near present-day Diamond Mountain Road, but only the hearthstone of their original home remains.[36]

Seeing a need and an opportunity, Dr. Bale hired an early settler named Ralph Kilburn to build and operate a sawmill that would furnish lumber for the burgeoning building projects in the area. The mill was built on the Napa River just north of the present-day town of St. Helena, where York Creek enters the river. This provided an opportunity for William and Henry to apply their carpentry skills in building yet another mill.

With the money they earned from building projects, the Fowlers acquired the means to branch out into ranching. By September of 1845, the Fowlers bought 4,000 acres of grazing land from Dr. Bale in the Upper Napa Valley.

In addition to the Fowlers and William Hargrave, less than a dozen other foreign men, some with families, moved into Napa Valley in 1845. Among them were John York and David Hudson, who later that year built the first cabins in what was known as Hot Springs. This would one day become the town of Calistoga, at the north end of the valley, a mile north of the Fowler's cabin. The main trail up the valley ran along the foot of the hills. The trail is now known as Foothill Boulevard, but for many years it was called Main Street. The York and Hudson cabins were built where the current-day Lincoln Avenue meets Foothill Boulevard.

Upper Napa Valley and Mount Saint Helena

The Upper Napa Valley had long been home to the Central Wappo people, who used the natural hot spring waters for healing and spiritual rituals. There were three Wappo villages at the north end of the valley when the Fowlers arrived, and the Native Americans remained on the land during the early period of Euro-American settlement. Much of the labor done on the Fowler ranch was carried out by Native Americans. The Fowlers' attitude toward the Wappo people was better than that of some of the other settlers. They did not abuse their indigenous neighbors and treated them fairly as workers. Nevertheless, the Fowlers also held an all too common sense of superiority over the local inhabitants and were said to have looked down on them generally. Perhaps most egregiously, they participated in the land grant system which essentially robbed the Wappo people of their land.

In the summer of 1846, John York and David Hudson vacated their cabins at Hot Springs and took their families to live in the somewhat more established town of Sonoma. The Fowlers and Hargrave, in turn, took up residence in the York cabin, and they would use it as the headquarters for their ranching operations over the next twenty years. Within a short time, the Fowlers had become one of the major landowners in the valley along with Dr. Bale and George Yount. Taking their cue from General Vallejo, William and Henry began to build up their herds of cattle and horses and to participate in the tallow and hide trade. They called their ranch "Fowler & Sons," and their home and ranch would be the nucleus of the future town of Calistoga as people moved onto the Fowler lands to live and work.

7

The Battle for California and the Bear Flag Revolt

Not everything was peaceful as the Fowlers sought to establish their lives in Alta California. By 1846, the relationship between immigrant Americans and the local Californios had become increasingly tense. Mexico and the Californios were sending mixed signals about the status of foreigners and their right to own land in California, and this, predictably, made the foreign settlers nervous. From the Californios' perspective, there were a growing number of able-bodied foreigners who knew how to use rifles, and therefore posed a threat to their authority and control in the region. Over time, the Mexican military garrisons, barracks, and presidios had fallen into disuse, and the Mexican soldiers had never been well trained or organized in the first place. If an armed conflict arose between the Californios and the new immigrants, the Californios knew they would lose.

A few months earlier, Captain John C. Fremont had been ordered by the United States to take a scientific expedition to California. He was also advised that, because of tensions with Mexico, he should be ready to turn his expedition into a military force if needed. The presence of Fremont and his men only added to the Californios' anxiety about a possible foreign takeover.

Unbeknownst to everyone living in California, hostilities between Mexico and the United States had already started. After Texas formally joined the United States at the end of 1845, American troops were sent to defend the new and disputed border along the Rio Grande. Mexico responded, and on May 13, 1846, the United States declared war on Mexico, starting what would become known as the Mexican-American War. In those days, word did not spread quickly from Washington D.C. to the Pacific Coast, and so American Consul Thomas Larkin in Monterey would not know about the declaration of war until months later.

In early June, William Hargrave, along with a few other Americans from Napa Valley, rode out to Captain Fremont's camp north of Sutter's Fort. Their intention was to express their concerns about the threats being made by the Mexican government and to ask for Fremont's help. Other Americans from the Sacramento Valley had also converged at Fremont's encampment. Fremont did not make any specific promises, much to the disappointment of his audience, but he seemed willing to support provoking the Californios into making the first move. Henry Fowler later recounted that he had heard that Fremont "advised them to go and take Sonoma" and assured the immigrants they would have "the best backing in the world."[37]

Given that both the Californios and the foreign settlers were on high alert, every incident had the potential to be interpreted as an act of aggression. Californio José Castro, the Commandante General of Alta California, sent a small group of men to drive a herd of horses toward Sutter's Fort. Many foreign settlers had gathered not far from Fremont's camp near the Sutter Buttes. Upon hearing of the approaching Californios, a group of several foreigners went south to intercept them. On June 9, the two groups were camped just two or three miles from each other. It was a tinderbox waiting for a spark.

The next morning, the foreigners surprised the Californios and captured their horses. They gave back a few and sent the Californios off with a message for Castro. If Castro wanted the rest of his horses, he would have to come and get them. More significantly, the foreign settlers related their plan to take over Sonoma and Sutter's Fort, thereby seizing control of the entire northern frontier of Alta California. Understandably, the Californios were alarmed by this substantial escalation of hostilities.

Having announced their takeover, the foreign settlers rounded up twenty men from the Sacramento Valley and headed toward Sonoma, using a back route via Napa Valley. They were led by William Ide and Ezekiel Merritt.

On June 12, the group stopped in Napa Valley with its concentration of American settlers. There, at the new grist mill being built on Dr. Bale's land, they met for two days to map out their capture of Sonoma.

People from all around the valley were also present, including William and Henry Fowler.[38]

While William Hargrave was keen to join the advance on Sonoma, William and Henry Fowler were less enthusiastic, perhaps due to their close working relationship with General Mariano Vallejo. Moreover, William was 67 years old, and he may have felt it was an enterprise better suited to younger men. Henry Fowler later wrote that, at the time, he thought there were enough men in the party, and he decided to ride in the following day after the seizure of the town to see how things had gone. In the end, about twelve Napa Valley residents joined the Sacramento group including William Hargrave, Sam Kelsey, Benjamin Kelsey, Andrew Kelsey, David Hudson, and Peter Storm.

Around midnight, the thirty-two men rode over the Mayacamas Mountains and down the neighboring valley to Sonoma. They arrived in the small, sleepy town just before sunrise. The barracks of Sonoma were no longer run as a military outfit, so little resistance was expected. General Vallejo was woken up by the sound of men gathering outside his home, and he quickly dressed. Vallejo's demeanor was hospitable as he invited several of the rebel leaders into his home to discuss matters, but he soon realized the gravity of the situation.

Vallejo had been sympathetic to the eventual takeover of California by the United States, so he likely had no objection to the rebels' goal of an independent California. His capture would have relieved him of any duty as a Mexican officer to resist an attack. Together Vallejo and the rebel leaders drafted and signed agreements declaring California an independent state. For a while it looked like the settler's revolt would be agreeable and peaceable.

Unfortunately, not all of the men who had been waiting outside Vallejo's home were content with the drafted agreements, and confusion among the insurgents broke out. It became clear that they had not thought through all the implications of capturing Sonoma, and despite the early morning hour, alcohol was a factor in the proceedings, contributing to the dissension. Caution was urged by the cooler heads, and fortunately for all, the morning passed without violence. However, despite the assurances implied in the making of the draft agreements, the rebels decided that Vallejo and his top men should be taken to Sutter's Fort rather than be released on parole.

A contingent of about ten men, including William Hargrave, escorted General Vallejo and a few other Californios to the fort. Like Hargrave, some men in the escort party had worked for Vallejo and knew him well. The mood was generally friendly, and the security was loose. Vallejo could still have expected to be released on parole after meeting with Captain Fremont. Vallejo even refused a rescue attempt on the grounds that it would make matters more difficult.

Contrary to expectations, when the party arrived at Sutter's Fort, they encountered a very different attitude from Captain Fremont. While he denied any responsibility for the arrests made by the rebels, he refused the prisoners parole and insisted on locking them up at Sutter's Fort with much less hospitality than Vallejo had shown the insurgents. Vallejo and his compatriots would remain imprisoned for almost two months in less than ideal conditions.

Back in Sonoma, the remaining rebels set about taking control of the town. They arrested a few more Californios, organized themselves into battalions, made a proclamation of independence, and raised a flag.

While most of the men who captured Sonoma were American, they had no official standing with the United States government and so could not raise the American flag. The situation called for a flag representing California's independence, and it seems that more than one flag was created.[39]

On June 13, Peter Storm crafted a flag at the Bale Mill gathering. Storm had been a sailor and was known for his handiwork, including sewing, painting, and heraldry designs. The cloth he used was said to have come from one of the women in attendance at the meeting such as Nancy Kelsey.[40] Red and white cloth stripes were sewn together and were likely meant to evoke the flag of the United States, or possibly the red and white flag of Texan independence. Using a chewed stick as a brush, Storm painted the image of a grizzly bear and a single blue star. The lone star was a nod to the flags of earlier independence movements. The grizzly bear was a common sight and was seen as a symbol of strength. Storm's grizzly stood on its hind legs on a patch of grass with its mouth open, growling for independence, as it were.

Henry Fowler recounted years later that he saw Storm's Bear Flag flying when he rode into Sonoma the next day. However, Storm's flag may have come down soon after. It seems that some people objected to the aggressive stance of the grizzly bear. Perhaps in response to this criticism, William L.

Todd, a cousin of Mary Todd Lincoln, made another flag with a grizzly bear on all fours. It seems that Todd's flag was made on June 14 and was based on Storm's design. It may have replaced Storm's flag on the flagpole later in the day or the following day. Todd's flag also received some criticism, as the less aggressive bear was said to look more like a pig. The current flag of California contains many of the elements of these early flags, including a star and a bear. The grizzly bear stands on all fours as in Todd's design, though the bear rests atop a patch of grass as in Storm's design.[41]

Peter Storm and the Bear Flag

This insurrection by the foreign settlers became known as the Bear Flag Revolt, and the thirty-two men who rode to take Sonoma were called Bear Flaggers. However, the Bear Flag did not fly for long.

News of the events in Sonoma spread rapidly. The Californios issued proclamations encouraging resistance to further rebellions and dissuading other foreigners from taking part in any conflicts. The Californios assumed that Fremont and the foreign settlers were acting on behalf of the United States, even though Fremont's role in the insurrection was ambiguous. While the initial revolt was accomplished without a shot fired, that would not be the case going forward. There were a few additional skirmishes north of San Francisco Bay, resulting in a couple of men dying on each side. Two of the first American casualties were Thomas Cowie and a man named George Fowler, who, despite sharing the name, was not related to the Fowler family of Napa Valley.

Captain Fremont and his troops arrived in Sonoma on June 25, eleven days after the Bear Flag Revolt, and Henry Fowler was on guard duty when the reinforcements arrived. The Californios realized that the American insurgents were too strong and too well armed to take on without reinforcements from the south, and so Fremont's advance met no resistance.

Fremont and a small group of men next traveled south from Sonoma, and on July 1, they assumed control of the village of Yerba Buena, later known as San Francisco. Fremont's men then returned to Sonoma to celebrate on the Fourth of July, which was a national American holiday by that time. On the following day, the Americans in Sonoma and Fremont's men officially joined forces to form the California Battalion. William Hargrave promptly joined Company C of the new California Battalion and was promoted to lieutenant, acting as a guide for Fremont.

Captain Fremont and the Bear Flaggers were not aware that the Mexican-American War had been declared in May, nor did they know that Commodore John Sloat had been commanded around that time to secure California's Pacific Coast on behalf of the U.S. government. On July 1, Sloat sailed into Monterey Bay, and on July 7 he landed his men in Monterey, the capital of Alta California, to announce the state of war and the annexation of California by the United States. The Mexicans had sent most of their men to Los Angeles in the south, and consequently, there was almost no one present to resist Sloat. The Stars and Stripes were raised that day without a single gunshot.

Two days later, Sloat's company raised the American flag over Yerba Buena, a mere eight days after Fremont's taking of the village. That same day in Sonoma, after just twenty-five days, the Bear Flag was lowered and the flag of the United States took its place.

Ultimately, the Bear Flag Revolt had no effect on the takeover of California by the United States. Political forces had been set in motion long before the Bear Flaggers rode into Sonoma, and the annexation of California was on track with or without the revolt. Despite this, there was a long-felt pride in the Bear Flag Revolt, and the Bear Flaggers were celebrated as heroes by locals for decades afterward.

Modern accounts of this period tend to offer a more balanced view of events, including the transgressions and injustices that took place during and after the revolt. For example, despite assurances, the Californios were not always treated fairly in the following years, often losing their land and livestock through squatting and theft. While it was not a policy of the United States to deprive Californios of their property, the fact was that Americans were frequently successful in their court challenges such that Californios often lost their landholdings. This attitude was by no means universal. Some of the earlier settlers continued to work with and support Californios, and a few Californios did retain their standing in the community, such as General Vallejo. However, in the end, the Californios not only lost control of their territory but many lost their homes and their legacy as well.

The California Battalion was officially made a part of the United States military, and local Americans continued to join up. Henry Fowler, who by then was a young man standing just under six feet tall, enlisted in August and accompanied the newly promoted Major Fremont when the battalion went south to San Diego. Within months, Henry broke his arm, and as a result, he never saw battle. He returned home to Napa Valley in November. Peter Storm also joined in early August and served for three months in Sonoma. Fighting continued throughout the year in Los Angeles and San Diego with thousands dying on both sides. The conflicts did not end in California until January 13, 1847, with the signing of the Treaty of Cahuenga.

Further south in Mexico, there were still more skirmishes for another year. The terms of the final 1848 Treaty of Guadalupe Hidalgo included a payment of 15 million dollars to Mexico for the formerly disputed territories, significantly less than the 25 million dollars the United States had offered before the war. The added land area was about the size of Western Europe and included what is now California, Nevada, Utah, Arizona, Colorado, New Mexico, and Texas, as well as parts of Oklahoma, Kansas, and Wyoming. In addition, the treaty delineated a new border between Mexico and the United States, and it gave Mexicans and Native Americans living in the ceded lands the option to move to Mexico or to receive full rights as citizens of the United States.

The fragility of governance on the frontier can be seen in the Bear Flag Revolt story. Being so far removed from Mexico's center of government, California had been left in the hands of competing Californio factions who were primarily focused on petty personal disputes. With no consistent enforcement of the law, the foreign settlers took their chances when participating in the land grant system, and they had to rely on the sometimes fickle relationships with those in power. Combined with the thin governmental infrastructure and a general lack of resources, it only required thirty-two armed men to declare Californian independence. Alternatively, it can also be said that independence was accomplished by a single U.S. naval ship sailing into Monterey Bay.

With treaties in place and California no longer in the war, life calmed down for the residents of the Napa Valley. Despite the tumult and shift in governance, the day-to-day workings of William and Henry's ranch and carpentry business continued much the same as it had under the Californios. Meanwhile, Bill Fowler had missed all the action in California as he was on his way back to Missouri to gather up the remaining Fowler family members and once again head west.

8

The Family Follows on the California Trail

———————•———————

During their stay in Sonoma at the end of 1844, the Fowler men hosted the explorer William H. Winter. The Fowlers had traveled with Winter from Missouri to Oregon in 1843 and from Oregon to California in the spring of 1844. Winter was planning to make the return journey overland to Missouri in the spring of 1845, and William and Henry were in favor of Bill joining him to bring back the rest of the family, along with some good cattle stock for breeding. This would be Bill's fourth sojourn between the United States and the Pacific Coast.

That same winter, the Stephens-Townsend-Murphy Party attempted to cross the Sierra Nevada Mountains into California guided by the mountain men Isaac Hitchcock and Caleb Greenwood. When the Stephens-Townsend-Murphy Party neared the mountains, a Paiute chief told them through gestures and drawings in the dirt that there was a river to the west that they could follow to cross the mountains. With no common spoken language between them, the party misunderstood the Paiute's name to be Truckee, and they used that name for the river up the east side of the Sierra. Traveling so late in the season, they were caught by snow while traversing the mountains. Some men pressed on to Sutter's Fort and then returned to escort the rest of the party to safety. In the spring, they returned to where they had left their wagons and managed to bring them over the mountains, making them the first party to take wagons over the Sierra. The Stephens-Townsend-Murphy Party's new and more direct route over the Sierra would

soon become the main route to the West, and it would become known as
the California Trail.

In May of 1845, Bill Fowler and William Winter hired Caleb Greenwood
and his two sons, John and Britton, to guide them back along this new
route. Bill and Winter had some difficulty gathering a group who wanted to
go east, but on May 12, they managed to leave Sutter's Fort on horseback
with fifteen men headed for Missouri. They were the first party to travel the
new California Trail crossing the Sierra Nevada Mountains from west to
east. There was still a lot of snow on the mountains as they passed through
the narrow notch that would later become known as Donner Pass. On
their way down the eastern slope of the Sierra, the Greenwoods improved
on the route by avoiding part of the steep Truckee Canyon and using a
bypass along Dog Valley. In the coming years, this would become the route
traveled by 250,000 pioneers headed to California.

Once on the eastern side of the Sierra, they traversed the deserts of the
Great Basin, vast areas with little or no vegetation. At times the water was
alkaline or so salty as to be undrinkable. The party arrived at Fort Hall in
present-day Southeast Idaho on June 20, and there Bill Fowler and William
Winter parted ways with the Greenwoods. A few days later at Soda Springs,
their party met up with twelve of Winter's colleagues who were making their
way east from Oregon. The chances of meeting up with familiar people in
such a vast wilderness were low, and the unplanned reunion was a happy
one. Several of the men decided to travel at a faster pace and separated
from the main group, while Bill and Winter stayed on with the seventeen
slower travelers. In early July, they came upon the vanguard of the 1845
wave of emigration that was headed west. They beheld what appeared to be
an endless line of wagons, with approximately 3,000 people scattered across
500 miles of trail.

Arriving at Fort Laramie on July 27, many of the men accompanying
Bill and Winter were tired after two and half months on the long, hard trail.
With around eight hundred miles still to go to their destination, ten men
decided to leave the party for the Missouri River so that they could travel
the remaining leg by boat. Bill and Winter, along with just five other men,
chose to continue on the California Trail, the most direct route back to
Independence, Missouri.

In Nebraska the group encountered tens of thousands of buffalo, once
riding ten miles through a vast herd. Some buffalo were almost seven feet

tall and weighed up to two thousand pounds. Winters wrote of the buffalo, "They were so thick, that, in many places, they blackened the earth for hundreds of acres."[42] In need of provisions, the small party spent time hunting a few buffalo and preserving the meat. They had to travel at night so that they could spend their days drying their catch in the sun.

Herd of Buffalo

As was common at the time, they had several interactions with Native Americans along the way. All of their meetings ended peacefully, despite their concerns about traveling as a small party. Some of the encounters required skillful negotiation, and once they felt the situation necessitated the threat of their guns. The following description of one such incident is based on the writings of William Winter and his colleague Overton Johnson.[43]

On August 13, along the Platte River in present-day Nebraska, a group of about fifteen men from the Pawnee tribe tried to stop the Winter Party. The Pawnee's pretense was that they were planning to hunt a large herd of buffalo the next day, and they did not want the pioneers to scare the buffalo that were in the next valley. The travelers doubted the Pawnees' story and decided to continue on. Not having successfully stopped the party from going ahead, the Pawnee men issued a signal which brought three hundred Pawnee in two columns running toward them at full speed.

Ambushed and outnumbered, the pioneers quickly calculated that re-treating, sheltering, or fighting were not prudent or possible. Their only course of action was to wait and hope to manage the situation, defending themselves as necessary. They stood back to back with their guns drawn as the Pawnee surrounded them. An old chief approached them with a folded piece of paper. The letter said the chief's name was White Man and that he had helped previous pioneers recover stolen goods. The letter further recommended that those who met the chief should give him presents. The chief then proceeded to tell them the same story about the planned buffalo hunt and asked them to come to the Pawnee camp for the night.

On the one hand, it seemed like it might be easiest for the small group to go along with the chief's request, given that they were surrounded and the note was somewhat convincing, if a bit unusual. However, with their homes and families not far away, the men decided they would stay the course. They firmly replied that they did not want to delay their travels and that they would be careful not to unsettle the buffalo. They even offered to let some of the Pawnee accompany them to ensure the buffalo were undisturbed. The chief reluctantly agreed to their proposal, and together they smoked and pledged their friendship. After offering the chief a few gifts, the small party left with twenty-two Pawnee men in tow.

All appeared to be well until the party stopped for the night and unloaded the horses, at which time the Pawnee men began to take everything they could. The pioneers were determined to stop them, and at gunpoint, they persuaded the Pawnee to put down the belongings. Winter's group re-packed their animals and sent the Pawnee away. One older Pawnee man followed them a short distance, telling the group not to stop for the night as some of the men "had bad hearts." They saw no buffalo on the trail ahead, and so to take extra care, the small party veered off the main trail and followed a parallel path.

There is no way of knowing how accurate this story is, and how it would be different if told by the Pawnees. What it illustrates is how the Americans interpreted the encounters they had with Native Americans and the stories they told about them.

Despite getting lost for a short while, Bill Fowler and his traveling com-panions eventually found the main trail again. Two weeks later on August 29, 1845, the seven men reached the Missouri border, after three and a half months on the trail.

After having been away for well over two years, Bill Fowler arrived back at the Fowlers' Missouri homestead in September of 1845. He had many stories to tell the family about the work he, Henry, and William had accomplished in Oregon building a mill and about their trip from Oregon to Sutter's Fort. Of particular significance was his description of what they found in California, especially the Napa Valley. His purpose would have been to entice Kitty Speed Musgrave and the whole Fowler-Musgrave clan to return with him to California. Having relocated to the frontier twice before, Kitty might have had an idea of the challenges such a move entailed, though each new frontier is unique and this time they would be relocating to a foreign country. The overland route to California would take about five months and cover two thousand miles across mountains and deserts. This would be twice as far as the journey from New York to Missouri and would take the family through areas that were much more remote and wild.

Altogether thirteen family members readied themselves for the expedition. Making the journey were Kitty and her new family: her husband Calvin, their four-year-old son James, and Calvin's younger brother Alfred Musgrave. Kitty's daughters would accompany them, which included Catherine and her husband, John Hargrave, along with their four young children, as well as Catherine's younger sisters Ann, age 15, and Minerva, age 13. In addition to his family, Bill was looking to persuade others to join them, and a notice recommending Bill as a guide for the trip to California appeared in the St. Louis and Independence, Missouri newspapers, describing him as "well acquainted with the route."[44]

The process of finding others to join an overland party was an informal one, and it was often based on families either knowing each other or finding some affinity like a shared religious background, a common friend, or simply getting along. Bill talked with neighboring families about the fertility of Napa Valley, convincing more than a few to come with him on the trek to California. Many of these St. Clair County families would settle near the Fowlers, including the Owsleys, Cyruses, Nashes, Kelloggs, and McDonnells.

To make the journey, everyone had to prepare to be largely self-sufficient, feeding and clothing themselves for five or six months. Every family would require a few well-made wagons, each with teams of four to six strong oxen to pull them. In addition, they would want to bring a few horses or mules, and at least one milking cow. Given that any of these animals might get sick or crippled along the way, it was wise to bring along extra animals if at all possible.

While the livestock would feed on the vegetation growing along the way, food for people was scarcer, and there were no towns for restocking supplies. It was recommended that each person bring two hundred pounds of flour, as well as some cornmeal, rice, bacon, dried beans, salt, sugar, baking soda, tea, and coffee. Though not guaranteed, those on the trail might be able to supplement what they brought with buffalo meat that the men could hunt along the earlier part of the trail.

Also on the list of necessities was cooking gear, including pans, utensils, and cups, as well as tents for sleeping and protection from the elements. The trail was tough on clothing, particularly boots and shoes, and those traveling west had to be prepared for scorching heat as well as freezing cold. The one opportunity they might have to procure items they needed was through trade with the Native Americans, and so the prudent pioneer would bring along extra shirts and various household items for barter.

Having fully stocked their wagons for the journey, Bill Fowler's group left their homes on April 30, 1846. They were headed for Independence, Missouri, located at the confluence of the Missouri and Kansas Rivers. The starting period for the overland journey west was restricted to April and May to ensure that sufficient grass had grown to feed the livestock along the trail and that the emigrants would have enough time to cross the Sierra Nevada Mountains before snows closed the passes in November.

The Fowlers were by no means the only ones going west. In 1846, Independence was the gathering place for about 1,500 people and 250 wagons headed for either Oregon or California. An equal number of emigrants also left from St. Joseph, about fifty miles north of Independence. The largest party going to California that year is known to history as the Russell Party. All told, the Russell Party would include about 130 men, 65 women, and 125 children with 72 wagons plus livestock.

In Independence, the Fowler group joined the Harlan Party with whom they would travel all the way to California, and Bill may have been hired as their guide.[45] The bond between the Fowler and Harlan families would become a lasting one. The Harlans were descended from Quaker immigrants who were a part of William Penn's colony in the late 1600s. This particular branch of the family had made multiple moves westward over forty years, settling most recently in Michigan.

Overland by Covered Wagon

The Harlan Party took its name from George Harlan, who was moving west with more than twenty members of his extended family. Others had also joined the Harlans on their way to Independence, including Peter Wimmer and his family and Heinrich Lienhard. Altogether, the Harlan Party, including the Fowlers, consisted of about twenty wagons, and they left Independence along with the Russell Party on May 12, 1846.

The emigrants formed into a loose confederation of parties, with alliances shifting as they traveled. Group leaders and rules were officially chosen in the first camp once everyone was on the trail. George Harlan felt the newly formed Russell Party, with over three hundred people, had grown too large to be manageable under a single leader. He contended that smaller parties would fare better, something that proved to be true. Harlan withdrew his name from consideration as a leader for the Russell Party and formed a smaller, separate party. The Harlan Party subsequently chose Judge Josiah Morin as their leader.

Groups mounted on horseback and with mule teams made better time than the slower oxen-pulled wagons and those traveling with herds of cattle, such as the Harlan Party. Many pioneers walked since wagons were often full of provisions and belongings and did not have sufficient suspension to cushion riders from the rough road. It was also advisable to lighten the wagon's load as much as possible to reduce the strain on the oxen. On the prairie, wagon trains covered ten to twenty miles a day. Traveling more than that would weaken the oxen, which could be disastrous. Further slowing their progress were challenging river crossings, wagon repairs, rounding up stray livestock, and the much-needed rest days for both people and animals. As a result, the parties traveled at varying speeds, often passing and repassing each other over the many months. The ill-fated Donner Party was among those in the Russell Party, and so the Fowlers may have met up with them occasionally as they moved from camp to camp.

The responsibilities men and women had along the trail were split along traditional lines. The women's days were filled with making and breaking camp, cooking meals, washing and mending clothes, looking after the sick, and caring for children. On the trail, Kitty's frontier skills would have come in handy, though there would have been even fewer amenities than in her earlier frontier cabins. Meals, for example, were cooked over open campfires and lit using flint rocks. At times there was no wood for the fires, and so buffalo chips and trash had to be used. Typical meals on the trail consisted of fresh meat, preserved meat like bacon, cornmeal mush and pancakes, beans and rice, milk, tea, coffee, and bread baked in a Dutch oven. One of the few tasks that were perhaps more easily accomplished on the road than at home was churning butter. The wagon did all the work as it bounced along with the butter churn tied to the side.

As grueling as the trip was for the women, it was equally demanding of the men. They drove the wagons, guided them over difficult passages, and performed the frequently required repairs. They would hitch and unhitch the oxen to the wagons, as well as herd and tend the other livestock. When the opportunity arose, the men would hunt game, such as buffalo, deer, and antelope. They would also handle the negotiations with Native Americans, and the disputes within their group and with other parties, which were often considerable.

Everyone had heard various stories about the Native Americans, most of which served to make them afraid of encounters with local tribes. However, even though the Sioux and Pawnee tribes were warring on the Plains at the time, they generally left the emigrants in the wagon trains alone. Occasionally, tribe members would offer to help with river crossings, and they often wanted to exchange goods. The moccasins they made were the only source of replacement footwear along the trail where even a few pairs of shoes and boots might not be enough for the whole trip.

Once the emigrants left Missouri and were out on the prairie early in their journey, they began to encounter a world quite unfamiliar to them. The ground was sometimes thick with hundreds of thousands of buffalo, and the sky stretched endlessly in every direction. To those familiar with the forests and rivers of the Eastern United States, this open and boundless terrain was an extraordinary sight. At some point, the sense of limitless expanse likely fueled the hopefulness many pioneers felt during the early stages of their travels.

As a relief to all the hard work, dust, mosquitoes, and boredom, the emigrants would gather around the campfire at night for dancing and music. The young folk would kick up their heels, dancing the Virginia reel and listening to popular melodies like "The Arkansas Traveler" and "Money Musk", an old Scottish tune. Ann Fowler was particularly noted for her violin playing. In a memoir, Jacob Harlan wrote:[46]

> *Every night we young folks had a dance on the green prairie. Our musician was usually a young fellow named Frank Kellogg, who played the fiddle pretty well, but from time to time, as our musician, we would get Ann Eliza Fowler. She was a young lady who afterwards became my wife, and in playing the fiddle she could just knock the hind-sights off Frank or any one in the train.*

Mrs. Wimmer concurred, saying, "[Ann Fowler] and her sister Minerva were expert violinists, and the character of music furnished the dancers was superb."[47]

Ann Fowler spent her sixteenth birthday out on the trail in present-day Western Wyoming. It coincided with the Fourth of July, a time of patriotic celebration even for those on a wagon train headed west. Jacob Harlan recalled the evening, writing that, after their usual dance, the young men stood in line with their guns to fire a salute into the air. He described how one young man had over-loaded his rifle in the hope of creating a louder noise and that when he fired he was knocked sixteen feet back while his rifle flew forty feet. The Fowlers were at the western edge of the United States and about to cross into Mexican Alta California, so the Fourth of July commemoration may have been accompanied by some mixed feelings: a sense of pride and growing nostalgia for the country they were leaving as well as some trepidation and excitement about what lay ahead.

Life on the trail was not easy, and the difficulties mounted as the miles wore on. The weather alone was a challenge and came in many forms: driving rain, lightning storms, searing heat, freezing cold, hail, wind, and the endless dust from the trail. In addition to the elements, there were numerous accidents, illnesses, and increasingly, exhaustion. While those traveling often focused their fear on Native Americans, in truth it was the daily afflictions that were the most dangerous and most liable to cut a pioneer's journey short. In the end, one in ten of the emigrants who set out from Missouri died along the way.

An anonymous letter published in newspapers that autumn described the despairing demeanor of the people arriving at the small fur-trading outpost of Fort Bridger, in present-day Southwest Wyoming:[48]

> *The emigrants were heartily tired of their journey, and nine tenths of them wished themselves back in the States. The whole company had been broken up into squads by dissatisfaction and bickerings, and it was pretty much every man for himself.*

9

A Perilous Passage

━━━━━━━ • ━━━━━━━

Two months and a thousand miles after leaving Independence, Missouri, the Fowlers and the Harlan Party reached Fort Bridger on July 16. It was here that they met up with Lansford Hastings, author of *The Emigrants' Guide to Oregon and California*. This popular guidebook had first inspired George Harlan back in Michigan to make the journey west. The guidebook had descriptions of the new frontier and "all necessary information relative to the equipment, supplies, and the method of traveling." Hastings also promoted a new shortcut across Utah, though his description was brief and vague:[49]

> *The California route, from Fort Hall to the Sacramento river, lies through alternate plains, prairies and valleys, and over hills, amid lofty mountains; thence down the great valley of the Sacramento, to the bay of St. Francisco [sic], a distance from Fort Hall, of nine hundred miles. The Indians are, in many places, very numerous; yet they are extremely timid, and entirely inoffensive. Wagons can be as readily taken from Fort Hall to the bay of St. Francisco [sic], as they can, from the States to Fort Hall; and, in fact, the latter part of the route, is found much more eligible for a wagon way, than the former. The most direct route, for the California emigrants, would be to leave the Oregon route, about two hundred miles east from Fort Hall; thence bearing west southwest, to the Salt lake; and*

thence continuing down to the bay of St. Francisco [sic], *by the route just described.*

This route, according to Hastings, would save emigrants between 200 and 400 miles, depending on the account. Constantly concerned about crossing the Sierra Nevada Mountains before the snows, this undoubtedly appealed to some party leaders.

Some doubted and warned against Hastings' proposed shortcut, but despite these cautions, about three hundred pioneers from the Russell Party decided to veer off from the main California Trail onto what would become known as Hastings Cutoff. The party leaders who were persuaded by the promise of a shortcut were George Harlan, Samuel Young, Edwin Bryant, Jacob Hoppe, and George Donner. Fortunately, several people would record their

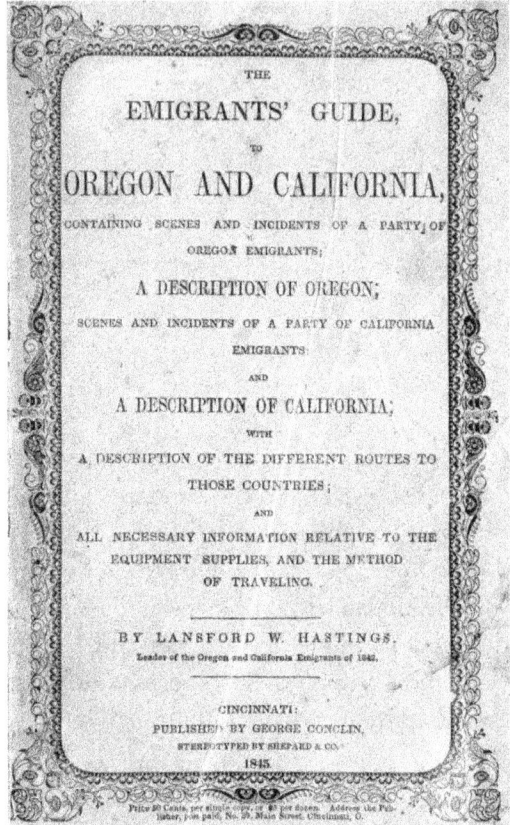

THE
EMIGRANTS' GUIDE,
TO
OREGON AND CALIFORNIA,
CONTAINING SCENES AND INCIDENTS OF A PARTY OF
OREGON EMIGRANTS;
A DESCRIPTION OF OREGON;
SCENES AND INCIDENTS OF A PARTY OF CALIFORNIA
EMIGRANTS;
AND
A DESCRIPTION OF CALIFORNIA;
WITH
A DESCRIPTION OF THE DIFFERENT ROUTES TO
THOSE COUNTRIES;
AND
ALL NECESSARY INFORMATION RELATIVE TO THE
EQUIPMENT SUPPLIES, AND THE METHOD
OF TRAVELING.

BY LANSFORD W. HASTINGS,
Leader of the Oregon and California Emigrants of 1842.

CINCINNATI:
PUBLISHED BY GEORGE CONCLIN,
STEREOTYPED BY SHEPARD & CO.
1845.

Hastings' Guide for Emigrants

respective trips on the cutoff in diaries that provide much of the detail for this part of the Fowler family story, particularly James Reed of the Donner Party, Edwin Bryant, and Heinrich Lienhard. The various independent parties loosely traveled together and totaled some forty families and over sixty wagons.[50] Compared to the other groups, the Harlan and Donner parties were much larger and included most of the wagon teams.

Remarkably, when Lansford Hastings published his guidebook in 1845, he had never actually traveled the shortcut he was recommending. After publication in the early part of 1846, Hastings did travel east from Sutter's

Fort generally along the path Captain Fremont had taken in 1845 and roughly the path he recommended to the westward wagon trains. Significantly, Hastings traveled without wagons. Hastings' lack of first-hand knowledge would become painfully evident time and again as the parties attempted what was essentially an uncharted path.

On July 20, 1846, Hastings guided the Fowlers and the Harlan Party, the Young Party, and their forty or so wagons out of Fort Bridger. Hastings' partner, James Hudspeth, led Bryant and eight other men on horseback with mules, along a slightly different route.[51] Other parties who decided to travel along the Hastings Cutoff continued to arrive in Fort Bridger after July 20. The dozen or so wagons of the Hoppe Party would soon set out to follow the Harlans without a guide.[52] The Donner Party would not reach Fort Bridger until July 27, and after resting their oxen and making repairs for four days, they too would follow the wagon tracks of the Harlan and Hoppe Parties on their own.

A few days later, Hastings left the Harlan-Young Party to continue on their own while he returned to assist parties that might be behind them on the trail. This started what would become a cascade of chaos. In Hastings' absence, Hudspeth met the Harlan-Young Party at Echo Canyon, and despite the difficulties he had encountered leading his party on horseback through Weber Canyon, he directed the wagon trains through this same territory. Why Hudspeth thought this was the best way to go is not clear, as it was not the route Hastings had intended.[53]

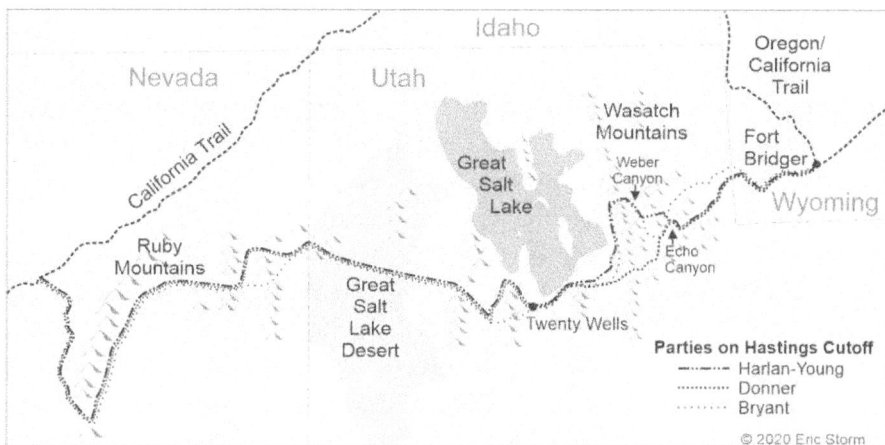

Map of Hastings Cutoff

Weber Canyon cuts through the Wasatch Mountains to the Great Salt Lake, but there was a five-mile section in which the steep gorge consisted of sheer drops and was littered with large boulders. The Harlan-Young Party spent six days of back-breaking work building a crude road, lifting the wagons over the rocks and lowering them down steep sections. Finally, on the seventh day, the group made it through the canyon.

On August 6, the Donner Party reached the mouth of Echo Canyon and found a letter Hastings' had stuck to a bush. Rather than waiting for Hasting to return as the letter instructed, three men, including James Reed, followed the wagon tracks down the canyon to find him. They all met on August 8 next to the Great Salt Lake. Upon seeing the difficulties they would encounter in the canyons, James Reed feared they would lose too many of their wagons in the process, and with advice from Hastings, Reed decided to go another route.

Regrettably, by taking the time to confer with Hastings, the Donner Party had been delayed another four days. Having successfully navigated down Weber Canyon, the Fowlers and Harlans reached the Great Salt Lake in the early days of August. The Donner Party would encounter yet more obstacles and miscommunications on their alternative route such that they would not reach the Great Salt Lake until two weeks later. These delays would, in the end, prove disastrous for the Donner Party.

Good things also happened along the Hastings Cutoff. The Harlan-Young Party was happy to have made it through the latest ordeal, and according to Jennie Wimmer, "For the first time in many weeks, there was music and dancing in the camp."[54] On August 6, 1846, they were camped near the Jordan River at a crossing that became known as North Temple in present-day Salt Lake City. There, Bill Fowler, 29, married 16-year-old Malinda Harlan, who was George Harlan's niece.[55] This was Bill's second marriage and the first of many nuptials between the Fowlers and Harlans.

A couple of days later, the Fowlers and the Harlan Party made it to Twenty Wells, now known as Grantsville, on the south side of the Great Salt Lake. There they rested and replenished water supplies for the trip across the desert. This break from the hard work of moving the wagons through Weber Canyon sadly came too late for 27-year-old John Hargrave, Catherine Fowler's husband. Exhausted from the previous week's toil, he died there of pneumonia on August 11, leaving Catherine and their four children to make the rest of the journey on their own. The following day,

John Hargrave was the first emigrant to be buried in what would become the state of Utah. A member of the Donner Party, Luke Halloran, would die in the same place two weeks later. He was buried next to Hargrave on August 25 in "a beautiful place," as James Reed of the Donner Party described it in his diary.[56] In front of the Donner-Reed Memorial Museum in Grantsville, Utah, there is a historical plaque titled "Utah's First Emigrant Graves" in remembrance of these two men.

The solemn funeral left a cloud over the party as they finalized their preparations for the desert trail ahead. Hastings told them there was a forty-mile stretch of the Great Salt Lake Desert devoid of water and vegetation. In fact, this barren trek turned out to extend for eighty miles. Making matters even worse, the wagons sank into the ground's salt crust more deeply than the mule train had, making the wagon train's progress even slower.

Edwin Bryant, who crossed the Great Salt Lake Desert on horseback just ahead of the Harlan-Young Party, wrote:[57]

There was no voice of animal, no hum of insect, disturbing the tomb-like solemnity. All was silence and death.

Great Salt Lake Desert

Virginia Reed of the Donner Party described this country in equally somber tones:[58]

> *A dreary, desolate, alkali waste; not a living thing could be seen; it seemed as though the hand of death had been laid upon the country.*

After three days of hard travel across the salty plains, Hastings came to tell the Harlan-Young Party that he had misjudged the distance and that they still had twenty-five miles to travel to reach water. Upon hearing the news, the party unhitched many of their wagons and drove their thirsty livestock to the springs at the western edge of the desert. Bill Fowler lost the oxen from two of his wagons when they ran off. His fellow travelers, the Kelloggs, generously gave him some of their precious oxen, a life-saving act. After all of the oxen were allowed to recuperate for three days, they were led back to retrieve the wagons.

Hastings' route continued to prove slower than anticipated. He led them south around the Ruby Mountains on what was essentially a one-hundred-mile detour. Finally, they returned to the main California Trail at the Humboldt River, near present-day Elko, Nevada. In the end, the Harlan-Young Party had spent over a week longer on the Hastings Cutoff than if they had stayed on the main trail, despite the route being seventy miles shorter. By contrast, the emigrants who had taken the regular route were at least seventy-five miles and a week or two ahead of them.[59]

George Harlan realized that the provisions for his group were low and that the few remaining oxen were too weak to haul the wagons over the formidable Sierra Nevada Mountains. He decided to send someone ahead to Sutter's Fort to bring back supplies and fresh oxen. George chose his 18-year-old nephew Jacob Harlan, who was the brother of Bill Fowler's new bride, Malinda Harlan. Bill Fowler sent along a letter for his brother, Henry, telling him that they had lost some stock animals and asking Henry to bring replacements. Accompanying Jacob on his ride was another young man named Tom Smith.

By this time, many emigrants had already made their way across the Great Basin, and some of them had had violent and deadly confrontations with the Native Americans living along the Humboldt River. As the Fowlers and Harlans made their way across the future state of Nevada, they had to contend with traveling in the wake of these hostilities. Ever vigilant, they kept their animals close and stayed armed as they forged ahead.

The local Native Americans likely saw Jacob Harlan and Tom Smith traveling by themselves as an easy target. The young men were attacked twice and fought back, reportedly killing some men from the local tribe. Making good time on horseback, Jacob and Tom eventually caught up with the emigrant party ahead of them. The group was led by former Missouri Governor Lilburn Boggs, with whom they had traveled on an earlier part of the trail. Jacob told them of his party's plight, and arrangements were made for a man to stay behind and wait for the Harlan-Young Party with seven hundred pounds of flour and some bacon. With some small sustenance for his family secured, Jacob continued with Tom over the mountains as his uncle had directed.

Upon reaching Sutter's Fort, Jacob showed John Sutter a letter from George Harlan appealing for assistance and outlining what they needed. Unfortunately, Sutter was unable to provide him with the needed supplies, but he did write a letter requesting provisions from a German named Captain Cordura, who lived north of Sutter's Fort. Before leaving the fort, Tom Smith announced that he would not be going back across the mountains to help the Harlan-Young Party. Smith wanted to join Fremont's forces who were heading south to fight against the Californios. Jacob was

Sierra Nevada Mountains

unable to convince Tom to change his mind, but he was determined to make it back to his family on his own if need be. Fortunately, Captain Cordura was willing to help Jacob and gave him a new horse and twelve good oxen. In addition, Cordura sent two Native Americans with Jacob as guides and extra labor to help the Harlan-Young Party cross the mountains.

On the way back across the Sierra Nevada, Jacob met two members of the Donner Party who had similarly been sent ahead for supplies. While Jacob felt unable to spare any resources for them, it may have been encouraging to them to see that Jacob was able to obtain fresh animals. One Donner Party member would be successful in bringing food and needed goods back to their group, but unfortunately, that would not be enough to keep them from the fate that awaited them.[60]

Jacob finally met up with the Harlan-Young and Boggs Parties as they were ascending the east side of the Sierra Nevada in Truckee Canyon. About the same time, Henry Fowler also showed up with some strong mules. It was a heartfelt reunion indeed. With the help of the fresh oxen and mules, the party made it over the mountains with little trouble.[61] However, their sense of accomplishment was short-lived, as on the way down into the Sacramento Valley another member of the Harlan Party died. The grief of the occasion probably overshadowed any sense of the group's good fortune at having finally reached California.

On October 24, at the foot of the mountains just before the land broadened into the wide valley floor, the party finally arrived at Johnson's Rancho, just a couple of days' ride north of Sutter's Fort. The next day, it rained heavily at the rancho while the precipitation fell as snow high in the mountains. The Fowlers along with Harlan-Young and Boggs parties were the last people to make it over the Sierra Nevada Mountains that year. The snows that began on October 25 started what would become one of the most severe winters on record. The massive snowstorm trapped the Donner Party in the mountains for months, and after much hardship and death, only forty-eight of the eighty-seven people survived.

George Harlan paid Captain Cordura for the oxen, which may have been the one thing that kept the Fowlers and others from becoming holed up with the Donners. He repaid Cordura with oxen he had brought from America. This pleased Cordua considerably, as the oxen could be bred to improve his own stock. The Harlan family continued to Sutter's Fort and then on to Mission Santa Clara, located at the south end of the San

Francisco Bay about one hundred miles southwest of the fort. Sadly, by this time, many in the group had contracted typhoid fever from the poor sanitation and hygiene afforded them on the trail. Symptoms included fever and general weakness, and it was so common among the emigrants that it was known as "camp fever" and "emigrant fever." George Harlan's wife Elizabeth and a couple of his other relatives soon died at Mission Santa Clara, just a few weeks after arriving in California. Their deaths were yet one more tragedy of the trail.

The members of the Harlan-Young Party had been through a lot together, but once in California, they went their separate ways as families and small groups. The Wimmers decided to stay at Sutter's Fort, which would prove to be a fortuitous decision on their part.

The Fowlers continued to Napa Valley, arriving in November 1846, five and a half months after leaving Missouri. One can imagine the relief and joy upon reaching the valley and reuniting the whole family. William and Henry had built a cabin across the valley from their own for Kitty, who was to live there with her husband and son, along with Catherine, her four children, and Ann and Minerva. After such a long time camping out on the trail, a place to call home must have felt very welcoming. The family would have much to catch up on as they filled each other in on the events of the past three and a half years.

It was not uncommon for people who knew each other to travel west together and then settle in the same area, thereby recreating some of the community they had before. This was true for the Fowlers as well, who found themselves surrounded by some of the same neighbors they had in Missouri. The families of the Owsleys, Cyruses, Nashes, Kelloggs, and McDonnells became well-known in Napa Valley as generations of their descendants played a significant role in upvalley history.

From Mission Santa Clara, George Harlan would move the following spring to nearby Mission San Jose, in the present-day town of Fremont, where he would start a small dairy with his eight surviving dairy cows. The Californios bred their cattle for the hides and tallow, and not for milk or meat. Immigrants like George brought with them different breeds that helped improve the local stock. George's second daughter, Mary Ann, worked in the dairy making butter, which sold for fifty cents a pound. She also cared for George's blind 91-year-old mother-in-law, who had remarkably survived the long trip overland from Michigan.

When these pioneers set out from Independence, Missouri, in May, they were heading to Mexican Alta California, a foreign country. By the time they arrived in November, they found themselves in California, a territory recently seized by the United States. The Mexican-American War was still being fought far to the south when they arrived, and Major Fremont was recruiting young men to fight in the battles. Some of the newcomers, including Jacob Harlan, joined Fremont and the California Battalion for a few months. Kitty's husband, Calvin Musgrave, and his brother Alfred also joined the California Battalion and served with the Mounted Riflemen of Company E under Captain John Grisby. Alfred was thrown from his horse and injured his hip in December before they reached the battlefields of Santa Barbara and Los Angeles. Fortunately, by January of 1847, the fighting had ceased, and all of the new immigrants could get on with the business of settling in California.

10

Buildings and Wedding Bells

———————— • ————————

While Bill Fowler was traveling with the rest of Fowlers from Missouri to California, William and Henry Fowler, along with William Hargrave, continued working on various building projects throughout Sonoma and Napa valleys. One such project was Bale Mill located one mile south of Calistoga, begun in 1846 and completed in 1847. While mills were critically important for providing wheat and corn flour, they were also the center of community life, where people frequently gathered to share news as they waited for their grain to be milled. The mill was a major resource center as well, including a large storehouse for grains and other supplies.

Dr. Edward Bale imported the millstones from France and shipped machinery via China at great expense. The structure was built as an over-shot mill powered by an elevated wooden flume carrying a stream of water to the top of a thirty-six-foot water wheel which turned as the water poured over it. The wooden wheel was an impressive sight, taller than most man-made structures in the area at the time. The Kelseys were millwrights and likely designed some of the complex machinery for processing the grain into meal and flour. The Fowlers and William Hargrave did the carpentry, working with hand tools to shape the local Douglas fir and coast redwood trees used for the project. Florentine Kellogg fabricated the ironwork and operated the mill. Everyone was paid for their efforts in the form of land from Dr. Bale's rancho. Other expenses were paid by Dr. Bale from the money he had received from the Fowlers' earlier land purchase. The mill

© 2020 Eric Storm

Bale Mill in Napa Valley

was built to last, and even after many years of inactivity, it was restored to working order starting in the 1960s and became part of the Bale Grist Mill State Historic Park, next to Bothe Napa Valley State Park.

The Fowlers also continued building for General Vallejo, the biggest landowner in the area, working on many of the General's properties. Most of these buildings had been constructed in the Spanish style, using adobe brick for the walls and wood for the window frames, doors, roof structures, and floors. The buildings were often two stories tall and configured to enclose a large courtyard. They featured covered wooden porches on both floors facing the internal courtyard. Since the buildings were mostly complete by 1843, William was likely employed for his skill at finish carpentry and joinery, crafting furniture, doors, and window frames.

In the town of Sonoma, William worked on the military barracks used as General Vallejo's headquarters and for storing supplies. The barracks were located next to the Sonoma Mission, which was the last mission established by the Spanish in California in 1823. William was also hired to do finish carpentry work on *Casa Grande*, Vallejo's impressive home situated next to the barracks on the plaza in Sonoma.

Sonoma Plaza in 1851 showing Vallejo homes, barracks, and mission

El Palacio, now known as the Petaluma Adobe, was the center of Vallejo's vast ranching enterprise, located in the valley to the west of Sonoma. The purpose of the building was to process and store huge quantities of tallow and cowhides, most of which were eventually shipped to the Eastern United States. Built as a large two-story structure around a huge courtyard, it was actually a small village that housed, fed, and serviced all the ranch workers numbering in the hundreds, and sometimes the thousands. As the Petaluma Valley is generally cooler than Sonoma in the summer, it was also where Vallejo and his guests stayed to escape the summer heat.

In early 1847, William and Henry Fowler worked on the Petaluma Adobe, doing what would turn out to be the last of the carpentry work done there. Later in 1889, General Vallejo wrote in a private letter describing the Petaluma Adobe, "Mr. Fowler, father of Mr. Henry Fowler, of Napa was the last carpenter who worked at my old house."[62]

In the winter of 1846-47, Lilburn Boggs, the former Governor of Missouri, and his family were staying at the Petaluma Adobe as guests of General Vallejo. On the California Trail, they had traveled alongside the Fowlers and the Harlan Party part of the way, and it had been Boggs who graciously left food for the Harlan-Young Party after their shortcut debacle. Many years later in 1910, his son, William Boggs, wrote a letter to a newspaper recalling the Fowlers' work.[63]

> *The carpenters were yet at work on the interior. The late Henry Fowler of Napa and his aged father, William Fowler Sr., were the men or carpenters employed to do the finishing work in the building which was a large square building with a court on the inside (the usual Mexican or Spanish style.)*

William Boggs went on to mention William Fowler making a cradle for his wife, who had just given birth to their first son.[64]

> *Mr. Fowler Sr. made a fine redwood cradle for Mrs. Boggs which was a very nice finished piece of carpenter work. The madame expressed her fears as to its durability, the work was so finely executed. The old gentleman said it would last to rock all the children she would have, and it was kept in the family until the baby it was made for grew up and had children of his own and they were also rocked in it.*

Ex-Governor Lilburn Boggs would later become the first *alcalde*, or mayor, of the district of Sonoma, making him the main American legal authority in the area, handling land sales, trials, and marriage ceremonies.

In 1850, Vallejo ordered a grand wooden house from the East Coast to be shipped in pieces around the Horn of South America to serve as the centerpiece of his new estate in Sonoma. *Lachryma Montis*, Latin for Mountain Tear, was named for the spring that flowed out from the hillside. The building reflected the showy Carpenter Gothic style, making it one of the most ornately decorated homes on the West Coast at the time. William Fowler worked on this project too, including finishing the interior wood-work and the staircase.

During their initial years in California, the Fowlers were not just building homes, they were also creating families. In the ten years following their arrival in California, each of the five Fowler children married and had children of their own. All of them, except for Henry, married someone from the Harlan family, underscoring the great bond that had formed between the two families during their travails on the California Trail.

The first Fowler-Harlan marriage was when Bill Fowler married Malinda Harlan on the journey west. On that same trip, Jacob Harlan, Malinda's brother, became smitten with Bill's younger sister, the blue-eyed Ann Fowler, who was considered the belle of the family. In his memoirs, Jacob wrote a detailed account of the plans he made to win her hand, demon-strating the eternal nature of love and courtship.

Upon arriving in California, Jacob went off to fight alongside Major Fremont in the south. When he returned, he undertook a lucrative job and earned the sizable sum of $520. He knew his sister Malinda would put in a good word for him as a suitable marriage partner for Ann, but he

Lachryma Montis, home of General Vallejo

wanted to leave nothing to chance. He suggested to his uncle George Harlan that he marry Ann's older sister, Catherine Fowler Hargrave, who had been widowed on the trail to California. George and Catherine were well acquainted, as he had led the party with her and the Fowler family across to the West. At the age of 45, George was also widowed, his wife dying shortly after arriving in California. As a woman of 26 with four young children, Catherine would likely have been looking to remarry. Jacob's matchmaking was successful, and a month later on August 1, 1847, George married Catherine and then moved from Mission San Jose to Hot Springs to join her family on the Fowler ranch.

Even after George had married into the Fowler family and could be counted on to support Jacob's marital ambitions, it took Jacob another two months to work up the courage to propose. When he did, he rode to the Fowler home in Hot Springs where, feeling weak in the knees, he summoned the nerve to knock on the door. Ann, who was aware of his intentions, opened the door and smiled. Encouraged by this, Jacob proceeded to ask if she would be his bride. Even though Ann and her mother, Kitty, were in favor of the match, Jacob still had to request Ann's hand from her father, William Fowler, who Jacob characterized as a "stern old Scotchman."[65]

Jacob Harlan quickly rode the forty miles from Hot Springs to Sonoma where William was working for Vallejo. William was gruff at first until Jacob more fully introduced himself. Immediately William warmed to him, remembering that Jacob had been the young man sent ahead to bring back food and oxen for the safe passage of his family over the Sierra. William said he admired Jacob's "pluck and perseverance," though he also remarked that he thought Jacob and Ann were too young to marry. Having come too far and invested too much to give up easily, Jacob answered that the problem would soon remedy itself as he and Ann grew older together after marriage. With a "grim smile" William gave his consent, adding that Jacob should "take care of [Ann and himself] and not depend on [William] for much help." Jacob said he was "young and strong, and not afraid of work, and could well take care of the girl and [himself] too." They then discussed arrangements for the wedding.[66]

Early the next morning, a very happy young man rode back to Hot Springs with the good news. Jacob Harlan was 19, and Ann Fowler was 17. They were married in Sonoma on November 22, 1847, with about a dozen guests in attendance and Lilburn Boggs officiating.

Before their marriage, Jacob had completed a large contract to deliver lumber to Yerba Buena, soon to be called San Francisco. It had been a family affair with Jacob, his uncle George, cousin Joel, and other in-laws cutting shingles and fence posts from the redwood trees in the hills above Oakland. Mary Ann Harlan Smith later recollected, "At that time there was nothing at all but oak trees where the city of Oakland now stands."[67] They sold the lumber at a good profit to William Leidesdorff who owned City Hotel, the first and only hotel in the growing town.[68]

In late 1847, Jacob used his money from the lumber venture to go into business with his brother-in-law and Ann's brother, Bill Fowler. They planned to open a livery stable in Yerba Buena, offering an important service in a new town where horses were the main form of transportation. They would hire out horses, wagons, and buggies, and also board horses for people visiting the area. They also sold hay, grain, and other products. Because livery stables were noisy, smelly affairs, they were often built on the edge of town. Jacob bought a piece of land at the corner of Union and Dupont Streets, north of the town center. Dupont Street was the main street of Yerba Buena and was originally named *Calle De La Fundacion*, or "street of the founding." Later it was renamed Grant Avenue, after President Ulysses S. Grant, and it runs through Chinatown and North Beach. Building lots were one-sixth of a city block, or about nineteen thousand square feet.

Jacob paid $150 for the property, $75 upfront and the balance six months later. Bill Fowler brought his family's carpentry skills to the undertaking and built the stables. With the purchase of fifteen saddles for their horses, Jacob and Bill were in business.

With their new venture located in Yerba Buena, Bill and Jacob rented a house nearby on Union Street where they could live with their wives. Not long afterward, George, Catherine, and her children left Napa Valley to join them. For all of them, this would have been a very new experience. The Fowlers and Harlans had moved two thousand miles from their frontier farms on the edge of the plains to a small town located on the Pacific coast. Everything, from the natural environment to the way of life, was unlike anything they had encountered before. They were experiencing a completely new world, one which was about to dramatically change beyond anyone's wildest imaginings.

11

Gold Transforms California

———•———

At the beginning of 1848, Yerba Buena was just a small town of about eight hundred souls. While the settlement sat strategically at the mouth of a large bay, its sandy hills, frequent wind and fog, and scarce fresh water had kept it from growing quickly. Generally, people preferred the climate and natural resources found in the other communities surrounding the San Francisco Bay. Upon first seeing what was then just a village in 1846, one of the Harlan daughters wrote:[69]

> At last we reached Yerba Buena, as San Francisco was then called. Several of us went ashore with the captain and a Mr. Clark, who settled in San Francisco and gave to "Clark's Point" the name which it still bears. There were no wharfs then, and the mud flats reached far out into the bay. We went ashore in a small boat.
>
> Yerba Buena was a village of a few shacks and one good-sized building built among the sand hills. At this time there were a number of Mormons there, two hundred having landed from the ship "Brooklyn" in July. The Mormon women seemed delighted to see us, following us all around.

At that time, the Spanish-built mission was more than two miles away from the *pueblo*, or village, of Yerba Buena. The original Spanish fort, the

San Francisco before the Gold Rush

presidio, was located a distance from the village as well, and both the mission and presidio were in decline. The port, however, was one of the best in the region, and Yerba Buena was destined to grow in both size and significance.

Initially, like most Spanish settlements, the pueblo grew up around a plaza, now known as Portsmouth Square. At the start of 1848, sixty school-age children were living in town, and some parents complained that there was no school for them to attend. This was quickly addressed, and on April 3, 1848, the first school in San Francisco, as it had recently been renamed, opened on the southwest corner of the plaza. Catherine Fowler Harlan's school-age children were among the students in what was the first public school in California.

Jacob Harlan and Bill Fowler's livery stable was off to a promising start as well. Jacob had asked William Leidesdorff to send guests from his City Hotel to their stable, which Leidesdorff did quite happily. Soon Jacob and Bill had sailors from the ships in the harbor renting horses for $2 for a half-day. The pair made an impressive $60 on their first day. After just three weeks, Jacob bought out Bill's share of the livery business. However, a couple of months later, at the request of his uncle George Harlan, Jacob took on George's son Joel as a new partner.

George Harlan owned property at the corner of Bush and Dupont, currently just outside the Dragon Gate to San Francisco's Chinatown. Today an alley at that spot bears the Harlan name. He had brought his dairy cows to San Francisco, and he ran the city's first dairy with his son Elisha Harlan. By early summer, George and Catherine had their first child together, Sarah Ann Harlan, who was born on June 21, 1848, in San Francisco.

Some have claimed that Sarah Harlan was the first child born to American parents in San Francisco. While technically that may be true, since both parents were American-born and Sarah's birth occurred after the town's name had been changed to San Francisco, it is also the case that many other children had been born there by that time. Some children were born to Spanish parents, some to Native American parents, and some to parents of mixed heritage. Jacob Leese, an American, and his Mexican wife, Maria Rosalia, who was the sister of General Vallejo, were early inhabitants of Yerba Buena. Their daughter, Rosalia Leese, was born in Yerba Buena in 1838. Two daughters of Englishman John Calvert Davis and his American-born wife, Elizabeth Ann Yount, the daughter of Napa Valley's George Yount, were born in Yerba Buena in 1845 and 1847, respectively.

While the historical significance of Sarah Harlan's birth is up for debate, the happy occasion was somewhat overshadowed by much bigger news and events of the day.

In the spring of 1848, the Harlans received a letter from "Uncle Peter." Peter Wimmer had previously been married to George Harlan's sister Polly. After Polly's untimely death in Missouri, Peter had remarried, but the familial connection had remained strong. George had convinced Peter and his new wife to join him on his journey to California from Missouri. Since his arrival, Peter Wimmer had been working for John Sutter, most recently on a sawmill on the American River in the Sierra Nevada foothills. The foreman on the job was James Marshall, and Wimmer was the head of the construction crew.

In late January 1848, Marshall and Wimmer were inspecting a newly deepened tailrace where the water flowed out from the sawmill. In the water, Marshall saw a gold-colored nugget.[70] Peter's wife, Elizabeth Jennie Wimmer, who cooked for the crew, boiled the nugget in a pot of lye she used for making soap. This was an old method for testing gold, something she had learned in Georgia where she had lived as a girl. In fact, she was the only one present who had ever seen real gold. The next morning, Mrs. Wimmer reported that the nugget had been unaffected by the caustic lye and that it appeared to be gold. To be absolutely sure, James Marshall had the nugget tested several different ways at Sutter's Fort. Much to everyone's excitement, the tests confirmed its genuineness. When Marshall and Sutter returned to Coloma, Marshall gave the nugget to Jennie Wimmer, saying it would make a nice ring. That first nugget is known to this day as the Wimmer Nugget, and it is kept in the Bancroft Library at the University of California, Berkeley.

Peter Wimmer's letter telling the Harlans of the discovery of gold urged them to come quickly. Of course, the Harlans were not the only ones to hear this remarkable news. Despite trying to keep the story quiet, word of the discovery was reported in the San Francisco press. On March 15, 1848, the newspaper *The Californian* ran a short article about the gold found at Sutter's sawmill on the American River. Understandably, there was some skepticism of such an incredible claim. Despite the doubt, news about the gold continued to spread quickly by word of mouth. After receiving Uncle Peter's letter, the Harlans told their friends and family, including the Fowlers and others in Napa Valley.

CALIFORNIAN

BY B. R. BUCKELEW,

SAN FRANCISCO, MARCH 15, 1848.

GOLD MINE FOUND.—In the newly made raceway of the Saw Mill recently erected by Captain Sutter, on the American Fork, gold has been found in considerable quantities. One person brought thirty dollars worth to New Helvetia, gathered there in a short time. California, no doubt, is rich in mineral wealth; great chances here for scientific capitalists. Gold has been found in almost every part of the country.

Notice of the Discovery of Gold

On May 12, 1848, in the San Francisco town plaza, the owner of one of the newspapers, Samuel Brannan, waved a bottle of gold dust and yelled, "Gold! Gold from the American River!" Of course, by then, Brannan had stocked his store with as many goods as he could get to sell to all the would-be miners.

With Brannan's declaration, the Gold Rush started, and everyone's plans changed almost overnight. During the next few months, the populations of towns shrank, sailors left ships abandoned in San Francisco Bay, and businesses closed as people rushed to the foothills of the Sierra Nevada Mountains. The school in San Francisco, which had just opened months before, closed when the teacher left for the goldfields. Both of the newspapers in San Francisco shut down operations, and so by June 1848 the town was without a paper.

The editors of *The Polynesian*, a newspaper from Honolulu, Hawaii, complained about the loss of news as newspapermen in California wrote of nothing other than gold. On July 15, the paper described the gold fever's impacts:[71]

> *The whole country is in a state of turmoil and every body is flying to the gold region to reap a fortune. All the seaport towns are deserted. Out of a population of nearly 1000, San Francisco only contains about 50 or 60 souls and these would leave were it possible.*

The Polynesian article went on writing of the effects in Hawaii:

> *The little city of Honolulu has probably never before witnessed such an excitement as the gold fever has created. Probably not less than 200 will leave for California in the course of two months, if passages can be procured. There will many mechanics and good citizens doubtless leave; but at the same time we shall rid the community of some whose presence is not particularly desirable. "It's an ill wind that blows no good." If we suffer the loss of some good citizens, we shall also get rid of many bad ones. We doubt not many will better their worldly condition; but it is impossible to foretell the final result.*

Those already in California and the West Coast had a distinct advantage. Being the first to reach the goldfields meant that some of them did quite well while the pickings were easily available. It took time for word to reach back East, and when it finally did, it was too late for people to make the overland journey that year.

Being among the first to hear the news, Jacob Harlan was quick to act. He told his wife, Ann, who was four months pregnant, and his cousin Joel that they should put the livery stable in San Francisco on hold and set up a store in the hills where gold was found. Jacob secured a loan from his friend William Leidesdorff and bought $4,500 worth of food, coffee, tea, shoes, picks and shovels, pans and kettles, and ammunition. They left immediately for Sutter's Fort by boat and then took an oxen team to Coloma, the site of Sutter's Mill and the discovery of gold. They stayed with Jacob and Joel's Uncle Peter until they built a log cabin and opened their store. Their highly-priced goods were in great demand, and soon they were being paid in small leather sacks of gold. Of course, Jacob and Joel Harlan also tried their hands at panning for gold, and they had some good fortune. In a single day in August, they pulled $1,600 worth of the precious metal out of the river.

Bill and Henry Fowler were also keen to profit from the Gold Rush. On April 11, 1848, Bill wrote to merchants in San Francisco to order goods to sell, describing that, while he was currently short of cash, he could promise to pay in full in just a month's time. Presumably, merchants were inundated with such requests, and it is unknown if Bill was granted his request.

Early that summer, the Fowler men, William Hargrave, and George Harlan went out together to search for gold. They first worked Bidwell's Bar on the Middle Fork of the Feather River. While Granville Swift, whom they had befriended on the way to Oregon in 1843, found a lot of gold at Bidwell's Bar, the rest of them only had modest luck there. With the price of everything being quite expensive, the group found it hard not to spend all the money they made. Looking for a more lucrative site, the Fowlers and George Harlan moved on to the American River near Coloma, not far from where gold was discovered. They tried the Middle and South Forks with somewhat greater success, but Hargrave was anxious to leave because of the Native Americans in the area. When they shifted their efforts to the North Fork of the American River, they finally hit pay dirt. Henry later said, "All we had to do was to kick over the dirt to find fine gold on the North Fork."[72] Their technique was to crevice the river bed, prying layers of rock away with knives, and then to pan the trapped sediments. Using this method, they were able to mine $1,000 to $1,500 worth of gold a day for several weeks. With their riches in hand, they headed back to Napa Valley.

George Harlan returned to the Gold Country at the beginning of August, bringing with him his wife, Catherine, their infant daughter, and the other older children, as well as his 93-year-old mother-in-law. They stayed near Catherine's younger sister Ann Fowler Harlan, who worked with her husband Jacob and Joel Harlan running their store in Coloma. Catherine, an experienced mother, was likely a comfort and help to Ann, who was pregnant with her first child. On September 9, 1848, Ann gave birth in Coloma to a son, Milton Howard Harlan.

As October came to a close and winter descended on the Sierra foothills, Jacob and Joel sold their store to Lansford Hastings, whom they knew from the ill-fated Hastings Cutoff. Hastings had recently opened up a store in Coloma, as had a few others who saw supplying miners a more sure bet than gold mining.

On their way back from the Gold Country, George's elderly mother-in-law died. She was laid to rest along the Sacramento River, and later it was said that she was buried where the California State Capitol now stands. This was not the only loss George and Catherine faced that year. Sometime during 1848 Catherine's oldest son William Hargrave died at the age of ten, which was, undoubtedly, experienced as a grave loss by the family.

Upon returning from the goldfields, everyone settled in for the winter. George and Catherine returned to the Fowler ranch at Hot Springs in the Napa Valley. Jacob and Ann moved to the Santa Clara Valley and the Fremont Hotel, which was owned by Jacob's older sister Sarah and her husband, George Washington Harlan. Sarah and George were first cousins, the children of two of George Harlan's brothers, and they had come west with the rest of the Harlan Party in 1846. (See the Harlan family tree on page 137.)

On December 8, 1848, William Henry Fowler III was born to Malinda and Bill Fowler. William would be their only child, and he would inherit his paternal line's desire to live his life on the frontier.

By the end of 1848, six thousand people had made their way to California to find their fortune. Men living in Oregon, Hawaii, Mexico, and Chile had relatively shorter journeys to make, and they were the next to arrive in the goldfields. Subsequently, as word spread around the world, people began flowing in by the tens of thousands. Over 90,000 people came to

Mining for Gold

California in 1849. They fittingly became known as the "forty-niners." Some of these forty-niners were said to have "gold fever," a lust for the shiny metal that led to poor or single-minded decisions. Many sold their farms, and some even left their families to seek riches in the foothills of the Sierra Nevada Mountains.

The trip from the East Coast of the United States to San Francisco took four or five months by ship traveling south around the Horn of South America. Crossing the Isthmus of Panama could make the trip a little shorter if there was a ship to catch on the Pacific side. The overland trip from Missouri similarly took four to five months. People also crossed the Pacific Ocean, leaving their homes in China and Australia in search of California gold.

Emigrating men far outnumbered women during the Gold Rush. On the frontier, this disparity was already common, but men made up an even greater portion of the throngs pouring into San Francisco and to what came to be known as the Gold Country. Of the 40,000 people who came by ship

to San Francisco in 1849, only 700 of them were women. There were concerns about the impact such an imbalance would have, and publications
were circulated back East encouraging young, educated women to come to
California to help civilize the hordes of men.

In early 1849, Jacob Harlan was itching to return to the Gold Country
and once again run a store selling goods to the flood of miners. His cousin
George W. Harlan, with whom he had been staying, was also keen, and so
they went in as partners on a wagon and ox team. In March 1849, Jacob
and George packed up their families and made their way to the Sierra
foothills. They stayed where the town of Columbia is now, a few miles north
of the town of Sonora. They bought a log cabin that had been a store and a
house, much to the relief of their wives, Ann and Sarah, who preferred the
relative comfort of a sparse cabin to camping in tents with the children.

While women were a rarity in the goldfields, children and families
were even rarer. Things like toys were in scarce supply, while gold coins
abounded. This would be the case for years to come, as the precious metal
continued to be the basis for exchange and people had sacks of gold squir-
reled away, quite literally for use on a rainy day. On those occasions, when
the children were stuck indoors due to bad weather, they might be given a
sack of gold pieces to play with in the absence of a set of wooden blocks or
other toys.

In addition to the store, Jacob and his cousin George spent some of
their time prospecting, and they were amply rewarded, finding thousands
of dollars worth of gold and gold dust. A month after they had arrived,
while they were out mining near Sonora, a Native American man came to
the log cabin where Ann and Sarah were living with the children. He spoke
enough English to warn them that twenty Native Americans were nearby in
the creek and that they were bad men who planned to kill them. He offered
to take the frightened women to where their husbands were working. After
the women hurriedly packed up the kids, they set off to find Jacob and
George. Upon seeing the panicked state of their wives, their husbands became concerned and angry. With $15,000 in gold in the cabin and no guns,
Jacob and George felt unprepared to defend themselves and their property.
George stayed with the women and children while Jacob rode to Sonora to
buy guns. Once armed, he quickly rode back to the cabin, only to find no
one there except the Native American man who had come to warn Ann and
Sarah. Jacob was relieved to have escaped misfortune and grateful for the

Minerva Fowler and Joel Harlan

man's help, and he gave him some presents for his trouble. The man seemed happy with the gifts, and one is left to wonder if there ever were any assailants in the creek.

In the tradition of Harlans marrying Fowlers, the youngest Fowler daughter, 16-year-old Minerva, became engaged to Joel Harlan. Joel was the 20-year-old son of George Harlan. Joel was also the cousin of Jacob, who was married to Minerva's sister Ann. Consequently, in addition to being cousins, Jacob and Joel were soon to be brothers-in-law. This would lead to quite a complex web of family relationships for them and their descendants.

Given his age, Joel had likely been interested in marriage sooner, but Minerva's father, William Fowler, probably had them wait until Minerva reached the age of 16. On April 2, 1849, Minerva and Joel rode from Hot Springs on horseback to Sonoma for their wedding. Alcalde Lilburn Boggs officiated, just as he had for Ann Fowler and Jacob Harlan. Not making it home before dark, the newlyweds spent their first night together camping somewhere on the rolling hills between Sonoma and Hot Springs.

In the summer of 1849, Bill and Henry Fowler, along with William Hargrave, returned to the same place on the North Fork of the American River where they found gold the year before. However, in the intervening months, the area had been well-mined by others. With the increasing competition, it was not as easy to find gold, and Henry had had his fill. The group soon returned to Napa Valley. Henry did make his way to the Placerville area the following year with a cousin, but they did not find much gold that year either.[73] In contrast, Henry's brother, Bill, never lost his interest in mining, and throughout his life, he would occasionally head out on prospecting trips hoping for the best.

Jacob and Ann, along with George and Sarah, remained in the Gold Country for the summer, and in the fall they all headed to Mission San Jose near where George and Sarah lived. Later that fall, Jacob and Ann, and Minerva and Joel finally returned to their livery stable business in San Francisco.

The Fowler-Harlan clan had done well in the Gold Rush. They each made thousands of dollars, most of which they invested in land, livestock, and businesses. This prudent use of their quickly gained wealth set the families up to prosper for decades to come. Gold had transformed California and Californians almost overnight. Had it not been discovered, California would likely have remained for many years a remote outpost for the adventurous American pioneers who lived there.

During his life, Dr. Edward Bale had many financial troubles, and before his death in 1849 he sold off most of his remaining land to the Fowlers. In April 1849, the Fowlers purchased the upper end of Bale's land grant for $800. The deed read:[74]

> *In the Valley of Nappa* [sic]*, as foresaid, Being a portion of the Ranch Calejolmanok Granted by the Mexican Govt. to E. T. Bale, that is to say, thirty-five hundred yards, Spanish measure, from N.N.E. to West S.W. in width and Six thousand, five hundred yards in length running S.E. & N.W. lying at the upper End of said Rancho: including the Hot Waters or Aqua Calientas.*

This addition of another 4,000 acres to the Fowler ranch meant that they owned almost the entire upper Napa Valley floor above Bale Mill, including the hot springs at the present site of the town of Calistoga. The following year they sold the 508 acres around the hot springs to Captain Matthew Ritchie and Reason Tucker for the sum of $10,000.

With the huge influx of people to California, land speculation became part of a second California rush. Jacob Harlan had been told to buy up city lots in San Francisco when they sold for just $10.50 each. Jacob, like the others in the Fowler-Harlan clan, had never lived in anything larger than a small country town, and he could not imagine the sandy hills ever becoming part of a wealthy city. He realized later that he could have become a very wealthy man had he followed that early advice.

Eventually, Jacob did get involved in some real estate business, once he saw how quickly San Francisco was transforming. On January 2, 1850, Jacob Harlan paid his cousin's husband $2,000 for a lot in San Francisco. While recording the deed at the Recorder's Office he was able to sell that same lot to Dr. Coit and his partners, making a $2,500 profit in just two days. However, not all land deals were so easy or straightforward.

George and Catherine Fowler Harlan had once owned the land on which San Francisco's Palace Hotel was later built in 1875. Before the Gold Rush, when George first heard about the lot, he had recommended it to Henry Fowler. Upon advice from his father, Henry passed on the purchase. Ultimately, Henry may have dodged a bullet, since the title to the land would eventually be forfeited in a legal controversy. Henry did own various lots in San Francisco, but, like Jacob, he was not confident in the value of the sandy tracts far from the town's center in what would become Pacific Heights, one of the wealthiest districts in the city. He later sold off these parcels for little or no profit. Henry would do much better in dealing with property he was more familiar with in Napa Valley.

George Harlan and Catherine moved back to San Francisco in March of 1850. George bought two lots on Green Street between Dupont and Stockton streets and relocated his dairy there. Soon afterward, his nephew and son, Jacob and Joel Harlan, took over the running of it. They employed Charles Gough at $150 a month to deliver the milk to the residents in the area. Gough was a forty-niner and the same age as Jacob and Joel. He had an old gray horse with one good eye, which he used to carry two large tin milk cans. Gough would ply the streets, measuring out milk to customers and returning to the dairy to refill the empty cans. On the first day, he sold $50 worth of milk, which worked out to $4 a gallon. Later Charles Gough would serve in an early volunteer firefighting organization known as the Vigilant Engine Company No. 9. He would go on to have a career in politics at both the city and state levels. Gough Street in San Francisco is named after him.[75]

Joel and Minerva Fowler Harlan, who had been married in the spring of 1849, wasted little time in starting a family. Their first child, Elisha C.

Harlan, was born on June 9, 1850, in San Francisco. With Elisha's birth, William Fowler and Kitty Speed Musgrave had seven grandchildren.

Catherine Fowler Harlan was also pregnant that spring after having lost a baby boy in infancy the previous year and losing her ten-year-old son the year before that. Not surprisingly, she took her four children from her home in San Francisco to her mother's in Napa Valley in order to have her baby.[76] It was during this time that her husband, George Harlan, became ill. He may have fallen sick during a visit to his daughter's home in Mission San Jose, or he may have gone there to convalesce. Sadly, on July 8, 1850, George Harlan died at Mission San Jose of typhoid fever, the same illness that had killed his first wife. Three and a half months later, Catherine gave birth to their son, George Harlan III, on October 27, 1850.[77] This must have been a tumultuous time for her, as she welcomed a new life into the world on the heels of her husband's death. Catherine, just 29 years of age, was widowed for the second time and had a newborn and four children to look after. She decided to stay with Kitty and Calvin Musgrave in Upper Napa Valley where she could raise her children with the support of her family.

In July, Jacob Harlan bought out his cousin Joel's interest in the livery stable and dairy, and he closed the livery stable to focus on the dairy business. He made good money selling milk at $40 a day. In October, Jacob sold eight of the cows for $1,200 and the dairy for $1,600. However, not all of his business investments were as successful. After selling the dairy, Jacob tried farming in San Jose, a venture that did not prosper and was short-lived.

It had been a tumultuous year full of the highs of good fortune and the lows of loss and death. Life for the Fowlers and others was shifting rapidly, as new opportunities quickly arose, and everyone sought to realize their ambitions and create a better life for themselves and their families.

12

Ranching at Hot Springs and Venturing to Hawaii

————— • ————

In December of 1849, William Fowler sold his share of their large cattle and horse ranch in Napa Valley to his son Henry Fowler for $6,000. Henry then partnered with his good friend William Hargrave to continue the venture under the name Fowler & Hargrave. Over the course of five

Cattle Ranching in California

years, they had become one of the major landowners and employers in the valley through their ranching and farm operations. William Fowler was about 70 years old at the time and was probably ready to pass the reins of their operation over to his son. Henry was said to be earnest, hard-working, and forthright. Despite his lack of formal education, he had grown into a competent businessman with notably good people skills, and the family business thrived in his hands.

Over the years, the Fowlers had received cash, land, and livestock as payment for their carpentry work. In one instance, Vallejo paid them with 300 cows and 50 horses for one of their jobs. They continued to build up their herds of cattle and horses, such that they eventually numbered in the thousands. These herds were spread over numerous ranches they had acquired in Napa, Pope, and Potter Valleys, each encompassing thousands of acres.

In the pastoral Mexican era, the value of cattle was in the hides and tallow. With the surge in population from the Gold Rush and so many new mouths to feed, the meat had become valuable as well. This resulted in a mini cattle boom for those like the Fowlers who had both cattle and land for grazing.

With every boom, there is a potential for a bust. In April of 1850, Henry and a group of men drove two hundred head of cattle to Sacramento near the Gold Country, where he hoped to sell the animals for $80 to $90 a head. However, good fortune was not on their side. Their efforts were thwarted by very heavy rains, and they had to swim with their cattle across flooded sloughs along the way. Despite getting very cold and very wet, all made it to Sacramento except one cow. Henry sold the cattle as a lot, but he was only able to get $40 per head in gold dust, a disappointing price and a decision he later regretted.

The Fowler's Napa Valley ranch not only had cattle and horses but also grew crops such

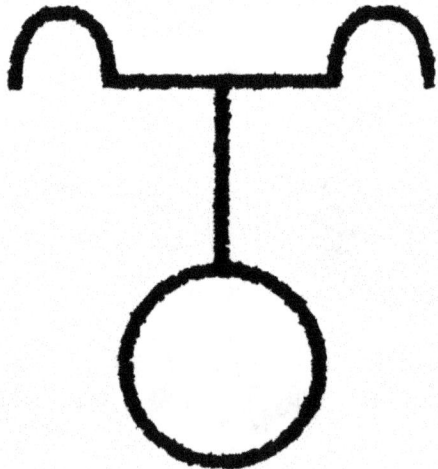

© 2020 Eric Storm

Fowler Cattle Brand

as wheat and hay. Kitty's second husband, Calvin Musgrave, and others worked on the ranch as farmers. The wheat they grew was brought by wagon to Bale Mill for grinding, and the miller would keep one sack of meal for every five sacks as payment for his services. The Fowlers also grew grapes in what was one of the earliest vineyards in Napa Valley, long before Napa became known for winemaking. Charles Krug was an early winemaker who arrived about this time in Napa Valley. He noted who was already growing grapes, some of which were made into wine with the rest used for eating. Krug recorded eight vineyards in the valley including Henry Fowler's one-acre vineyard in Hot Springs. Other landowners with vineyards included Yount, Bale, York, Hudson, Kellogg, Tucker, and Owsley, totaling just over a dozen acres.

The 1850 census shows less than one hundred settlers living in Upper Napa Valley. Through the 1850s, a town began to grow around the hot springs at the north end of Napa Valley. Still, it was a quiet place where everyone knew each other. The upvalley people were said to be industrious. They were involved in raising cattle and horses, farming a variety of grains, tending fruit and nut orchards, and cultivating vineyards that would later become world-famous. The Fowlers were well respected and an integral part of their community, and many people worked for one of their enterprises, bought or rented land from their holdings, or had business dealings with them.

Even though William sold his interest in the Fowler & Sons, he was by no means thinking of retiring in the conventional sense. He continued his involvement in building projects until late in life. One of the smaller noteworthy projects William undertook was in preparation for his inevitable death. Being the expert carpenter and joiner that he was, William built himself an airtight coffin made of rosewood, which he conveniently stored underneath his bed.

As California's population grew, William Fowler again cast his gaze toward a new frontier. He had gone as far west as he could in North America, so he next set his sights on the Hawaiian Islands. This move would take him further than ever before, landing him almost 5,000 miles from his home-town of Albany, New York. In February 1850, at the age of 71, William set sail aboard the American clipper ship *Fanny Forrester*, for the three-week journey to Honolulu.[78] William likely saw this as his final move, as he took his coffin with him.

The Hawaiian archipelago had united under the House of Kamehameha in the early 1800s, creating an independent constitutional monarchy recognized by the nations of Europe. When William arrived, 84,000 people lived on the Hawaiian Islands, of which approximately 1,000 were foreign-born. The population of Honolulu County on the island of Oahu was about 25,000. Honolulu was already an important trading center and whaling port in the middle of the Pacific when it became the capital of the Hawaiian Kingdom in 1845. The islands became further connected to the rest of the world by the introduction of a post office in 1850, and in that same year, foreigners were allowed to own land for the first time. In addition to the Euro-American immigrants, there were increasing numbers of Chinese men who had been recruited to work in the sugar cane fields.

Honolulu in 1850

Contact with foreigners had taken its toll on the native Hawaiians over the decades, as it had with other indigenous people. The native population had dropped dramatically throughout the 1800s, as Hawaiians became sick and died from the infectious diseases brought by the Euro-Americans. In just three years, while William lived there, the population of the islands dropped from 84,000 to 73,000. The area around Honolulu lost about 2,000 people, despite the arrival of an additional 1,000 foreigners.

Hawaii would not have felt like a completely foreign culture for William Fowler. He had worked with Hawaiians while building the mill in Oregon City seven years earlier. The Hawaiian Islands resupplied ships with food and water, and so they had been an important part of the Pacific sea trade between the Pacific Northwest, China, Britain, and the United States. The Hawaiians were excellent sailors and were often hired aboard Euro-American ships. It was not uncommon for the Hawaiians to stay in port cities on the west coast of North American working at a great variety of jobs. Hundreds of Kanakas, as the Hawaiians were called, worked for John McLoughlin at his sawmill, as pilots for boats moving goods, and at other skilled tasks. William would have also heard stories of Hawaii from those like Sam Brannan who had been there. Perhaps it was with some sense of familiarity that William headed to Hawaii.

William Fowler bought land and built thirty homes on speculation just outside Honolulu, in Palolo Valley near Diamond Head. He also bought land on Hotel Street in downtown Honolulu. However, with the population decreasing, there was not a lot of demand for new buildings. In the end, William's Hawaiian construction ventures were only mildly successful, and he found the climate did not suit him. In 1853, 73-year-old William returned to Hot Springs, with his coffin.[79]

13

Shifting Fortunes

———————•———————

California became the thirty-first state admitted to the United States on September 9, 1850. The population had swelled to 92,600, more than a ten-fold increase from 8,000 people just five years earlier. Two years later, a special state census would show a continuing explosion of growth to 261,000 residents. The Gold Rush had changed California forever.

The 1850 and 1852 census figures did not include the total population of Native Americans then living in California. Those figures would tell a different story as their numbers steadily declined throughout the 1850s, 60s, and 70s. As was true for many Native Americans, the indigenous people of California had no natural immunity to many of the diseases the foreigners brought with them. They also suffered and died from the many disruptions to their way of life, including the loss of traditional foods with the introduction of ranching. Native Americans throughout the state continued to be killed, abused, and marginalized as a result of state-sanctioned policies and the taking of land for gold mining, logging, farming, and ranching. Within a couple of decades of the Fowlers' arrival, less than one hundred Wappo people were living in the Napa Valley.

The range of attitudes and treatment Euro-Americans displayed toward the local inhabitants varied from respectful to abusive. The early Napa Valley pioneer George Yount was known for cultivating good relationships with his Native American neighbors. The Fowlers also were said to be fair in their dealings with them, though their attitude may best be described as humane, as opposed to respectful of Native Americans as equals.

At the other end of the spectrum was the Kelsey family, who had come to California with the Fowlers and who were known for their long-standing abusive treatment of indigenous people. The Kelseys were from Kentucky, a pro-slavery state, and they may have viewed Native Americans as they did African Americans. Andrew Kelsey, one of the four Kelsey brothers who came west with the Bidwell-Bartleson Party, and his associate Charles Stone had forced men from the Pomo tribe in the Clear Lake area, thirty miles north of Hot Springs, to work for them in what can only be described as a state of slavery. They were said to have abused local women and children as well. These practices were relatively common among the Californios and Spanish missionaries, who also used threats and violence to coerce the Native Americans into labor. Many Pomos died because of Kelsey and Stone's actions, and the tribe eventually retaliated. One morning in December of 1849, a few Pomo men attacked and killed Andrew Kelsey and Charles Stone, hiding their corpses by burying them.

When news of Andrew Kelsey and Charles Stone's deaths finally emerged many weeks later, Andrew's brothers, Ben and Samuel Kelsey, each led raiding parties in revenge. They threatened to "hunt and kill every Indian, male and female, in the country."[80] The indiscriminate slaughter did not happen at Clear Lake where Kelsey and Stone were killed. Instead, the men attacked Native Americans throughout Sonoma and Napa Valleys. The raiding parties burned indigenous villages, killing at least thirty people and chasing hundreds of others into the hills. The most deadly raid was on the Fowler Ranch, where the murderers shot fifteen innocent people. As a result of a complaint by a rancher, Sam Kelsey and six others were arrested for murder. Several men, including Ben Kelsey, were charged and released on bail, while others were named as being present at the murders but not charged.

The case of Sam Kelsey and his six co-defendants was the first-ever heard by the California Supreme Court, which was not yet fully established. It would be six more months before California was admitted to the Union, and consequently, the Court was unclear on its jurisdiction for charges against the seven who stood accused. The Court was not yet set up for trials, and there were no state jails if the men were sentenced. For these reasons, the Court released the men on bail until they were to stand trial in Sonoma.

Predictably, many of them promptly fled the area. Some of them moved to Humboldt Bay in the remote northern wilds of California, including Samuel and Ben Kelsey who took flight with their wives and children. After a couple of years, the Kelseys moved on and remained on the lam for the rest of their lives, continuing to harass and kill Native Americans and evading the law all the while.

Despite arresting Samuel Kelsey and the others for their deeds against Native Americans, that spring a U.S. military expedition was sent to Clear Lake to launch an official retaliation against the Pomo tribe. The military brought with them boats and cannons, and their subsequent onslaught is now known as the Bloody Island Massacre. The Pomo were trapped on an island where they had been hiding since learning that a significant force was coming to kill them. The U.S. military with their boats and superior fire-power attacked the island, slaughtering hundreds of people in just one day. The military's response was exceedingly disproportionate; in response to the deaths of two white men, hundreds of Native Americans were killed without due process. Such was the level of unequal treatment and persecution of the indigenous people of California by the U.S. government.

In 1852, Bill Fowler had a serious accident. As a result, he became partially paralyzed, and his speech and mental processing became impaired. In his written history of the family, Fowler Mallett attributed Bill's incapacity to either a stroke or a head or spine injury. Whatever the reason, this once handsome and dashing adventurer suddenly found himself profoundly diminished at the age of 35. While Bill's mind remained sharp in some ways, such that he was able to read the daily paper, his speech was greatly altered. He spoke in gibberish that was a blend of English, Spanish, and Native American and only somewhat comprehensible to those who knew him well.

Bill's injury may have caused or at least contributed to his wife Malinda Harlan Fowler filing for divorce and choosing to raise their son William III without him. The following year she would go on to marry Powhatan E. Edmundson, with whom she would have four more children.[81]

Bill Fowler spent the rest of his days dependent on and living with his siblings. He would periodically move between them, staying with either Henry or Minerva. At Minerva and Joel's property, Bill stayed in the bunkhouse, though it offended him to be housed with the workers on the ranch. Behind Henry's home, Bill had a cabin for himself, which he preferred.

To fill his days, Bill spent time doing the things he loved: hunting, fishing, and looking for gold.

In 1851, Jacob and Ann Fowler Harlan were among the first to settle in what became known as Squattersville, now called San Lorenzo, on the eastern shore of the San Francisco Bay. Squatting was a somewhat common practice whereby people would settle and work on an unoccupied portion of someone's land, especially when the holdings were vast and sparsely managed. The concept of land ownership arrived with the Spanish, who took the land from the Native Americans and then granted it to their citizens. Later, Mexico issued land grants to Californios and early European and American immigrants, such as the Fowlers. As California became an American territory and then a state, many of the people with these land grants had to deal with squatters and legal challenges to their rights of ownership in the U.S. courts. In the case of Squattersville, the land had originally been granted to two Californios, but the dividing line between their properties was unclear. Jacob and Ann used the land to grow potatoes and other vegetables and sold them at good prices to the rapidly growing population in the Bay Area. While living in Squattersville in April of 1852, Jacob and Ann had their second child, a girl named Mary Alice.

Ann's sister Minerva was also an early settler in Squattersville. In 1852, Minerva's husband, Joel Harlan, sold his interest in their farming venture to Jacob and Ann and moved his family ten miles east to the San Ramon Valley. Joel used his gold money to purchase land and build a modest house at a spot that would become the border of Alameda County when it was separated from Contra Costa County in 1853. After four years, Joel and Minerva traded their ranch for 1,040 acres nearby, and in 1858, they built a much grander home in the Gothic Revival style, which they called *El Nido*, or The Nest. There they created an attractive homestead with shade and ornamental trees and several outbuildings. Over time they purchased additional lands, and at one point their ranch encompassed 1,756 acres. Likewise, the house was expanded over the years, and it remained in the family for over 150 years.[82]

Joel successfully farmed and raised livestock in the San Ramon Valley, and he was well-liked in the community. In addition to raising nine children, Minerva was noted as a generous host and an excellent cook. The earlier Californios had been known for their abundant hospitality, and this openness to visitors was continued by some of the early pioneers who brought

El Nido and the Harlan Ranch in 1879

with them their own sense of Southern hospitality. Guests were always graciously welcomed, and they could anticipate sitting down to a sumptuous meal with all the fixings the hostess could muster. In addition to running the household, Minerva continued to enjoy the musical skills she had developed as a child, singing and playing the violin, guitar, and harp. She also cultivated her artistic talents, including painting landscapes and flowers.

By the fall of 1852, Jacob Harlan made plans for a trip to visit his childhood home in Indiana, a journey he detailed extensively in his published memoir. In moving to California, Jacob had been able to distance himself from his difficult childhood. His mother died when he was two years old, and he reports that his father's second wife was physically abusive. When he was ten, his father consigned him to live with his Uncle Elijah, who worked Jacob and his other children to the point of exhaustion and even death. At age 16, Jacob finally had the good fortune to be sent on to yet another uncle, George Harlan in Michigan, with whom he came west. At age 24, Jacob felt it was time to return to his family and show them the successful man he had become. He sold everything he had and paid off his debts, leaving him with the substantial sum of $8,500. His wife, Ann Fowler

Harlan, consented to the trip and stayed with their child at the home of her sister Minerva.

Jacob decided to travel to the East Coast via steamship rather than make the arduous and long trip across the country. While in San Francisco waiting to board the ship, he met his cousin George Washington Harlan along with a few other relatives and acquaintances were heading back East on the same ship. They all departed on November 13, 1852, aboard the brand new steamer aptly named the *Golden Gate*.

Jacob described the ship as luxurious, despite his being seasick for much of the voyage. The ship made its way to Panama, where Jacob and the group disembarked to cross the Isthmus of Panama by mule, boat, and train. They were met on the other side by the steamer the *Illinois* for the journey to New York. They arrived on December 12, just a month after departing from San Francisco. As he stepped off the boat, Jacob stepped into what must have seemed to him as the most populated place on earth since New York City had a population of over half a million people.

Jacob bought a fine suit for $65 to impress his Uncle Elijah. He then took the train to Indiana, where he hired an impressive carriage and horses for the remainder of the journey to Elijah's farm.[83] According to Jacob, his plan to dazzle Elijah and his wife Betsy succeeded, and they were astonished when they saw Jacob ride up in all his finery. Jacob took this opportunity to tell them how they had worked their own son John to death and had done almost the same to him. He said that, while he would forgive them, he would never forget how poorly they had treated him.

Having settled this score in his mind, Jacob set out to visit the rest of his family, who were equally surprised to see him. Over the next month, he met with people from his past, and because of his difficult childhood, some of the reunions were contentious, as Jacob was one to speak his mind. Jacob's sister Martha had died, and his only brother, Jehu, was in financial difficulty. Jacob was able to help out his brother, and he also bought his father's farm in Northern Indiana, leaving it to his favorite half-sister, Sylvina, once his stepmother died.

Jacob had intended to return overland to California bringing a herd of cattle with him. During his visit, many of his Harlan relatives and their extended families decided to go west with him. One family member to join him was Sylvina's brother and Jacob's half-brother, George Alonzo Harlan. George Washington Harlan and Samuel Street, who had made the sea journey to New York with Jacob, were also driving cattle back to California. They were accompanied by yet more Harlan family members, including George Washington Harlan's brother, William J. Harlan, and his family along with their half-brother and his wife, Elias and Elizabeth Draper, and their family.

Finally, in the spring of 1853, everyone packed up their belongings and set out for Missouri, some on horseback and some in wagons. There they bought supplies, more wagons, and hundreds of cattle to drive to California.

As with all overland journeys, this one had its fair share of hardships and tragedies. A young boy drowned during a river crossing when a wagon overturned, and Elizabeth Draper had a miscarriage while they traveled along the Platte River. The party also lost over a third of their cattle along the way, mostly from eating poisonous plants. They arrived in the San Joaquin Valley of California in September of 1853 after "five months and twenty-one days on the road from Omaha to Stockton."[84]

Upon his arrival in California, Jacob Harlan purchased land a few miles south of Stockton in the San Joaquin Valley, near the present-day town of Lathrop. He brought his wife, Ann, and children out from the San Ramon Valley, and set up a home and orchard. Soon Jacob saw the business opportunity in owning a ferry across the San Joaquin River, particularly one that offered the shortest route between Sacramento and San Jose. Jacob bought a half interest in Slocum's Ferry, later called Johnson's Ferry, for $6,000 which he paid for with land and cattle.

The ferry boat was operated by a team of horses on the river bank attached to cables to pull the ferry back and forth across the river. Realizing there was a sizable income to be made from the ferry service, Jacob bought out his partner for another $4,500. Eventually, Jacob was making $400 to $500 a month in fares, and double that amount during the State Fair in Stockton. In addition, Jacob collected $112 in monthly rent from his properties in San Francisco, and he owned a home and ranch land with three hundred head of cattle and twenty-five horses. This marked what was to be a career high-point for Jacob, who had arrived in California as a teenager and through his efforts had built up a prosperous life with Ann for himself and his family over the course of seven years.

Jacob and Ann stayed on at Slocum's Ferry for the next six years. During this time, Ann gave birth to three more children. Unfortunately, there is almost no record of what Ann's life was like. While Jacob's memoir is full of details about his activities, especially his business ventures, he offers few descriptions of his domestic life with Ann. He does appear to care for his family very much, wishing to protect and provide for them, and he mentions consulting with Ann about their life decisions. However, other than her musical talent and blue eyes, and the birth of their children, there is no specific description of what Ann's existence entailed.

By October of 1859, Jacob's health was poor, and a doctor told him to leave the damp Sacramento Delta lowlands for a drier climate. Taking his doctor's advice, Jacob traded his ferry for cattle and drove them down to Cholame Valley in San Luis Obispo County. Several of his Harlan relations, including his cousin William J. Harlan and William's half-brother Elias Draper, had gone to Cholame Valley earlier and had land for cattle. Jacob entrusted his herd to his half-brother, George Alonzo Harlan, and he returned to take Ann and their children back to Squattersville.

Having relocated to the eastern shore of the San Francisco Bay, Jacob purchased a squatter's claim from his cousin George Washington Harlan. The almost sixty acres of land was not far from where he and Ann had lived before in Squattersville, in present-day San Leandro. Eventually, Jacob also made a payment to the original rancho owner in an effort to secure the rights for his claim. This put Jacob in an awkward position. Since many of the squatters in the area still insisted on their rights to squat, Jacob drew ire from them by affirming the Californio owner's right to sell the land to him.

Meanwhile, community life in the Upper Napa Valley in the 1850s continued to evolve. Elizabeth Cyrus Wright offers a glimpse of the social life the residents enjoyed in her book *The Early Upper Napa Valley*:[85]

> *During their early years it was a strong social community, bright, attractive, high spirited young women and fine upstanding men. Many were the happy gatherings— quilting bees among women; and horse breaking contests and hunts among the men; an occasional house party at one or another of the homes and more or less rarely a trip to Sonoma (horseback of course) by a party of the more enthusiastic ones to a big "dance." Sonoma being the nearest approach to a town within reach and being a presidio, was well supplied with beaus who gave these attractive girls a good time and put the local men quite*

*on their best behavior to keep up. Such trips occupied
several days, the girls visiting in the hospitable homes of
the American families of Sonoma.*

In 1866, the *Daily Alta California* newspaper wrote:[86]

Pioneers.

> *No one part of the State can boast of so many pioneers
among its inhabitants as Napa. In the Upper Valley, most
all of the settlers are of long standing, and belong to that
little army of hardy adventurers that penetrated these
Western shores long before the discovery of gold. It is an
interesting sight to see, here and there, over [the] valley, the
log cabins that sheltered the pioneers of a State still young,
but mighty in her sudden growth. The earliest of all the
pale faces that settled this valley has now gone to that
"undiscovered country," but has left behind him the history
of a life, replete with heroism and high daring. George
Yount will ever be remembered as the dauntless pioneer—
the "Boone" of the Pacific. Among his early companion
settlers still living, are Captain Ritchie, Henry Fowler, John
Cyrus, the Gray family, and many others that I cannot now
mention. They have seen the valley transformed from a
wilderness to the quiet home of man, as if by magic.*

From the beginning, there were people of different faiths living in Napa
Valley. In 1853, the first church building was completed, and eventually, it
would come to be known as the "old White Church." It was meant to
function as a non-denominational church, though inevitably, there were
tensions among the churchgoers about sharing the space. The building
consisted of a simple rectangular structure, twenty-two feet by thirty-two
feet, with separate entrances for men and women. It was located near Bale
Mill on land that the early pioneer Reason Tucker had owned. The site for
the church was an obvious choice since Bale Mill was already the center of
the community.

Before the church was built, the Reverend Asa White had conducted
services at the site under a blue tent. The White Church was named for
him, though the building itself was painted white too. Upon its completion,

Reverend White continued to deliver services at the church for at least ten years. He later moved to the Methodist church in the town of St. Helena, three and a half miles down the valley. While everyone was free to share the building for religious services, community members of certain faiths would sometimes choose to ride long distances to attend a church of their specific denomination elsewhere. For example, the Cyrus family would ride almost twenty miles each way to Santa Rosa on summer Sunday mornings until a Baptist church was opened in St. Helena in 1857. Next to the White Church, there was a small cemetery, which was the final resting place for some of the earliest pioneers to the area. The church burned down in 1906, but the cemetery remains and is part of the Bothe Napa State Park.

Kitty and Calvin Musgrave's home and farm were at the north end of the Fowler ranch, between present-day Mrytledale Road and Lake County Highway. Their son James Musgrave, known as "Bud" in the family, was the youngest of Kitty's children and lived with her and Calvin in Hot Springs. Despite his physical challenges from achondroplasia, or perhaps because of them, James eventually became a teacher of Spencerian penmanship, which was the standard style of the day at a time when all documents were hand-written. He would also marry a neighbor girl and have a daughter.[87]

There were several Musgraves living in Hot Springs at the time including Calvin Musgrave's brother Alfred, their cousin Thomas, and his father Bennett Musgrave.[88] This abundance of family may have been what drew Lewis Musgrave, another cousin of Calvin and Alfred's to the area sometime after the Gold Rush. It was at Kitty and Calvin's home that Lewis met Catherine Fowler Harlan, who lived there with her children. Lewis was a large, strong, and charismatic 24-year-old man, who must have appealed to Catherine, who was then 35 and twice widowed. On May 14, 1856, Lewis H. Musgrave became Catherine's third husband in a ceremony in Hot Springs. Together, they would have three children: Edward, Ella, and Florina, born in February 1857, December 1857, and 1861, respectively.

The following year, Henry Fowler became the last of the Fowler siblings to tie the knot. On September 29, 1857, Henry, who was 35, married 16-year-old Catherine Magness. William Hargrave likely knew the Magness family from Arkansas.[89] In 1852, the Magnesses moved to California, and William Hargrave ran into them in San Francisco. As a consequence, the Magness family moved to Napa Valley, where they farmed land that was part of the Fowler & Hargrave ranching business.

Henry Fowler was not the only one looking to settle down. On April 22, 1857, in Napa, William Hargrave married Anna Collins.[90] Anna was born about 1838 in County Limerick, Ireland, and was twenty years younger than William Hargrave. They lived in their home on the Fowler & Hargrave ranch in Hot Springs, the home of the extended Fowler and Musgrave clans. At the time, this included William Fowler, Henry and his new wife Catherine Magness Fowler, Kitty and Calvin Musgrave and their son James, Catherine and Lewis Musgrave and their children, and Alfred Musgrave and his family. Only Ann and Minerva lived away from the ranch, sixty miles to the south in Alameda and Contra Costa Counties respectively. Due to his impairments, Bill Fowler alternated between living in the south with his sister Minerva and up north in Hot Springs with his brother, Henry.

While new families and new lives were flourishing for the Fowlers during this time, death was an ever-present and tragic thread running through their lives as well. Anna Harlan, one of Minerva's daughters, died on July 10, 1859, at the tender age of five.

Then, in 1862, the first of the Fowler siblings died. Catherine Fowler Musgrave passed away on January 9 in Hot Springs. She was 40 years old. Except for a brief time in San Francisco, Catherine had lived her whole life on the frontier. She was probably typical of pioneer women, marrying and having children from an early age, and spending the majority of her time tending house and raising children in somewhat sparse and challenging conditions. Over her life, she experienced the death of two of her children as well as two husbands, one of whom died while making the journey to California. Catherine was buried in the cemetery next to the old White Church. She was

Catherine Fowler Musgrave

survived by her husband Lewis Musgrave and eight of her ten children, who ranged in age from less than a year to 23 years old.

Even though Lewis Musgrave had three children with Catherine, he did not exhibit much interest in caring for his offspring once their mother died. He seems to have spent his time traveling to and from California buying and selling livestock and transporting supplies. While he did list Hot Springs as his residence in his 1864 Civil War Draft Registration, he does not appear to have provided an actual home for his children.

Before her death, Catherine's sons from her first marriage, James and Frederick Hargrave, had left home to live with their uncle Henry Fowler. They grew up alongside his younger children and were quite close to his family. It probably also helped that Henry's friend and business partner, William Hargrave, was a cousin once removed to James and Frederick.[91] The five younger children from Catherine's marriages to George Harlan and Lewis Musgrave, having become essentially orphaned, lived with their grandmother, Kitty.

Losing their mother and being abandoned by their father was surely difficult for the children, but Lewis Musgrave's exit from the family could be seen as a blessing in the long run. What Musgrave did once he left the Napa Valley deserves a more complete telling.

14

The Wild West and Lewis Musgrave

What came to be known as the Wild West represented the last phase of the frontier in the United States. During the first phase, the frontier lay in the mountains and valleys to the west of the colonial settlements on the East Coast. In the second phase, the frontier was pushed further west to the Mississippi River Valley. The third phase entailed the movement of a large number of people to the Pacific Coast of Oregon and California. The fourth and final phase of the frontier was different. At that point, the frontier relocated to the east, in the lands between the Great Plains and the Cascade and Sierra Nevada Mountains. These were known as the Western Territories, and they had remained sparsely populated as towns and cities sprouted up along the West Coast.

Despite how big the Wild West lives in the popular imagination as the story of the West generally, it only existed for about thirty years from roughly 1865 to 1895. It started as the Civil War ended and the Plains were opened up for cattle ranching. The enormous herds of buffalo that had once roamed the region had been hunted by Euro-Americans to near extinction. Into these wide-open spaces came people and cows, with devastating consequences for the Native Americans in the region. The newly completed transcontinental railroad brought new settlers into the interior of the country in search of land. The railroad also gave ranchers better access to the Chicago and Eastern markets for their beef. Eventually, cattlemen drove herds from as far south as Texas to the railways in Kansas and from as far north as the Dakotas to the rail lines that ran through Southern Wyoming. This movement began to wind down in the 1870s, as the open range was increasingly hemmed in by landowners using barbed wire to fence off land for their own use. By the 1890s, new farmland in the once spacious Plains had become scarce, and the steady flow of people to the American frontier finally came to an end.

The Wild West depicted by Hollywood was more a fantasy than a reflection of historic reality. Most towns in the West were quiet places settled by law-abiding citizens. There were even laws that restricted the carrying of guns in towns, and most people died not from bullets, but disease and old age. Outlaws, shootouts, and hangings were mercifully rare occurrences. All of which makes the deeds of Lewis Musgrave more remarkable.

Lewis Musgrave was born in Illinois in 1832, but his family moved to Tennessee when he was a young boy. Tennessee was the birthplace of his father, Thomas, and where most of his siblings were born. His mother, Sarah Elizabeth, was from Georgia. When Lewis was about 10 years old, the family moved again, this time from Tennessee to Panola County, Mississippi, where Lewis spent the remainder of his youth. Sometime in his twenties, Lewis left his home in Mississippi for California, likely arriving after the Gold Rush. Who knows what lured him west, but he did have family there. Kitty's husband, Calvin Musgrave, and his brother Alfred Musgrave were cousins of Lewis' father.

By January of 1862, Lewis was widowed with three children, and it was at this point his life seemed to take a turn for the worse. The American Civil War had begun a year earlier, and while California was a long way from the fighting, Californians sometimes took sides and even came to blows over the issue. Coming from the south, it is not surprising that Lewis Musgrave had strong sympathies for the Confederacy.

Sometime in 1862 or 1863, Lewis got into an argument with a man in Napa Valley over the merits of the Union versus the Confederacy. Lewis ended up shooting him, and he was run out of town. He is next reported to have killed two men in the Nevada Territory before moving on to Wyoming and Colorado. There he traded with the Native Americans for a short time. In 1863, Lewis Musgrave, or L. H. Musgrove as he was known by then, was arrested for murder at Fort Halleck, in what was then the Territory of Idaho. He had shot a man of European and Native American descent who had called Lewis a liar. Lewis was taken by the authorities to Denver for trial, but he was released from custody based on a legal technicality.

Having murdered both white and Native American men at this point, Lewis was no longer seen as a trustworthy member of either community, and he became an outlaw, living on the fringes of society. Outlaws could be quite brazen at the time, emboldened by the generally weak criminal justice system. There were large legal loopholes for criminals to slip through, and the jails were far from secure. Murder convictions were almost impossible to make as juries were sympathetic to men who claimed they were defending their honor.

Clearly living on the other side of the law, and without many legitimate options open to him, Lewis began to actively engage in horse and cattle rustling. The targets of his exploits were primarily government property. This may have been fueled by his resentment of governmental authority, but it also had the advantage of not antagonizing the local populace. Since Musgrave's thievery did not directly threaten the local ranchers' livestock, they were inclined to look the other way when the government's cattle went missing. In later years, his companions offered this account of how Musgrave had become a horse thief and outlaw:[92]

> *(It was an) act of retaliation on the United States government. Musgrove* [sic] *used to own a train of freighting teams and once ventured on the Indian reservation then lying about Laramie City. The government officials searched his wagon, and, finding whiskey, confiscated the whole train and threw the proprietor into the guard house. He was compelled to clean up the officers' quarters, cleaning spittoons and other such dirty work. When he escaped from this he went into the business of stealing United States property at every opportunity. His gang always claimed that they never stole anything from private citizens, but the record is not exactly clear as to this.*

While murder might be considered the ultimate crime, in the Wild West, stealing livestock was seen as nearly as villainous. Given the remoteness of the towns, supplies had to be brought in hundreds of miles using oxen, mules, and horses. Livestock was not only critical as a form of transportation but as a source of food as well. In this way, a horse or cattle thief was seen as life-threatening as a murderer. The monetary stakes were high as well. At a time when labor wages were just $2 a day for a man, a single mule was worth $200 to $300.

Lewis was smart and charismatic, and over time he pulled together a loose band of fellow outlaws who operated in many states and territories. Together they became known as The Musgrove Gang. The gang often disguised their thefts by impersonating Native Americans, who were suspected of stealing livestock generally. Using this tactic in the fall of 1864, they stole fifty head of cattle from Fort Steele, returning a short time later to take all of the cavalry horses. The soldiers went in search of the animals and the thieves, but to no avail. Newspaper accounts reported similar incidents in Colorado and Wyoming throughout 1867 and 1868.

The Musgrove Gang had various hideouts such as the narrow and rocky Poudre Canyon near Fort Collins in Colorado. The gang would alter or erase the brands on the livestock and drive the animals far enough to sell them without raising suspicion, often stealing more livestock on their return trip.

According to one newspaper, "the Musgrove gang ... was possibly the largest and most desperate lot of men that was ever joined together in the west for unlawful purposes. The members of the band were to be found in every state and territory—with the exception of three—west of the Mississippi river."[93]

Denver City Marshal David J. Cook described Musgrave as a formidable character:[94]

> *Musgrove* [sic] *was one of the marked villains of the pioneer days of Colorado, and as cool a character as it was ever the fortune of a detective or criminal officer to fall in with. He was a man of large stature, of shapely physique, piercing eye and steady nerve, who might have stood as the original for the heavy villain of the best story of a master in romance literature. He was a man of daring, inured to danger, calm at the most critical times—a commander whose orders must be obeyed, who planned with wisdom and who executed with precision and dispatch. He was the leader of an organized band of horse thieves, highwaymen and murderers, who infested the western plains, with Denver as general headquarters, during the*

years 1867-'68. They made the railroad towns a con-
venience in disposing of their booty, but did not spend
time in loafing about these places when there was other
and more profitable business to attend to in other places.
... (He) organized a band of horse thieves, which operated
throughout the entire plains country, and which was one
of the most formidable bands of desperadoes known to
frontier history. Musgrove was a perfect organizer. He had
his operators in Colorado, Wyoming, New Mexico, Texas,
Nebraska, Kansas and others of the western states and
territories, and carried on a regular business of stealing
and selling stock. They would drive off entire droves of
horses from one section and sell them in another five
hundred miles away, and would steal another drove in the
neighborhood of the late sale and drive it for sale back to
the place at which they had made the previous raid.

On October 25, 1868, near Elk Mountain, Wyoming, the Musgrove Gang attacked a mule train carrying wood for the railroad. All sixteen of the gang were dressed as Native Americans. They killed four men, scalping two of them, and drove off with sixteen mules. Three of the mule train men escaped and lived to tell the tale. Some say that nearby Bloody Lake was named for this incident.

Three days later, railroad man John Cronin spotted Musgrave, still in disguise, and gave chase for four miles. When Musgrave was caught he offered Cronin $200 in gold to let him go, an offer Cronin refused. Instead, he handcuffed Musgrave and bound his feet to take him to Fort Steele. On the train to Cheyenne, Musgrave complained that his foot bindings were too tight, and when they were removed, Musgrave jumped from the slow-moving train. As he was still handcuffed, his escape was hampered, and he was quickly recaptured. He was finally brought to Denver, Colorado, in a coach, escorted by forty soldiers. Lewis Musgrave was charged with stealing $100,000 worth of government livestock and the murder of the four men from the mule train, substantiating his status as one of the most notorious outlaws in the West.

Musgrave was put in jail to be held for trial. David Cook, the City Marshal of Denver, knew that Musgrave's men would try to bust Musgrave out, as was common in that era. Sure enough, after Musgrave's arrest, his right-hand man, Ed Franklin, and Sanford Duggan arrived in Denver. Both men had long criminal records, including charges for murder and breaking out of jail. The two men rode into Denver the night of November 20, and they proceeded to hold up three men on their way to see Musgrave. One victim was a judge who recognized Duggan from a trial for the assault of a prostitute. The judge pretended not to know his assailants in order to survive the encounter. The next day, he notified Marshal Cook of the holdup, but not before Franklin had visited Musgrave in his jail cell, no doubt to plan an escape.

On November 22, Franklin and Duggan were seen in the neighboring town of Golden, and Marshal Cook was notified. The description of what happened is like a scene out of a Western. That night, Marshal Cook and five of his men rode into Golden to bring the two criminals to justice. Duggan was in a saloon, but he managed to escape after a brief shootout with the lawmen, leaving the saloon owner fatally wounded. Franklin was in his hotel room nearby. Marshal Cook and his men tried to arrest Franklin, but he fought back saying, "I suppose you can kill me, but you can not arrest me."[95] Franklin made a move for a gun and was shot by two different men. Unable to find Duggan, the lawmen returned to Denver early the next morning.

Following Franklin's visit to see him in jail, Musgrave boasted that his escape was imminent and that his gang would soon set him free. By noon of November 23, the people of Denver were concerned Musgrave might once again evade justice, and they began to talk about taking matters into their own hands. Serving as both judge and jury, the people issued a verdict that Musgrave was guilty. By three o'clock, hundreds of people, including some of Denver's most respected citizens, had gathered and marched down Larimer Street to the jail. Once there, everyone seemed to be in agreement about their purpose, and no one objected when a vote was called to hang Lewis Musgrave.

The jailers offered no resistance as members of the public went to Musgrave's cell to haul him out. Lewis Musgrave stood there defiantly with a hastily made club. A few shots were fired, and Musgrave was subdued and brought out to the waiting mob. They took him one hundred yards to the Larimer Street Bridge over Cherry Creek, where Musgrave begged to be allowed to write two letters. What was going on in Musgrave's mind as he faced the belligerent crowd will never be known. Perhaps he was trying to persuade them to reconsider their verdict, or maybe he wanted to make sure he could offer his version of events for his family and posterity. Whatever the case, there on the railing of the bridge Lewis Musgrave penciled the following letters, as reproduced in a newspaper at the time:[96]

> DENVER, Nov. 23d, 68.
>
> MY DEAR BROTHER:
>
> I am to bee hung to-day on false charges by a mob my children is in Napa vally Cal—will you go and get them & take care of them for me god Knows that I am innocent pray for me—but I was here when the mob took me. Brother good by forEver—take care my pore little children I remain your unfortunate Brother
>
> good bie
> L H MUSGROVE
>
> The above was directed to W. C. Musgrove, Como Depot, Miss.

In addition to writing to his brother, Lewis wrote to his new wife. At some point in the intervening years after Catherine's death, Lewis Musgrave had married a young woman named Mary living in the Wyoming Territory. To her Lewis wrote:[97]

> DENVER C. T.,
>
> MY DEAR WIFE: Before this reaches you I will be no more, Mary I am as you know innocent of the charges made against me. I do not know what they are agoing to hang me for unless it is because I am acquainted with Ed Franklin—godd will protect you I hope good bye for ever as ever yours sell what I have and keep it.
>
> L. H. MUSGROVE.
>
> This was directed to Mrs M. E. Musgrove, Cheyenne, W. T.

As Musgrave was finishing his letters, men tied his legs together and brought a wagon around. Despite his bindings, Musgrave nimbly leapt into the wagon, and they drove under the bridge to a noose hanging from the

The Hanging of Lewis Musgrave

bridge. With the noose around his neck, Lewis Musgrave coolly rolled and smoked a cigarette, eyeing the crowd and probably still hoping for his gang to show up and rescue him. From the bridge above, a man tried to talk the public out of the lynching, but they could not be dissuaded and cried back, "Drive on!"[98] Musgrave's hat was pulled down over his face, signaling to Musgrave that there was only one way this was going to end. Feeling the wagon move out from under him, Musgrave jumped into the air to increase the weight of his fall and ensure a quick death. After five minutes, his hat was removed to show that he was indeed dead. Lewis H. Musgrave was just 34 years old.

Sanford Duggan, who had escaped in Golden, was later captured in Cheyenne. Despite the marshal's efforts to avoid another lynching, Duggan was also hanged by a group of citizens from the same bridge a week later. These grizzly events were enough to break up the Musgrove Gang for good.

Strangely, this was not the end of the drama of Lewis Musgrave. His body was likely buried in Denver's Mt. Prospect Cemetery near the outer edge, a section reserved for outlaws, criminals, and the poor. Due to the cemetery's association with these less savory characters, the wealthier citizens of Denver began to favor the Riverside Cemetery, and Mt. Prospect Cemetery, or "Old Boneyard" as it was also known, fell into disuse and disrepair. With an eye toward redevelopment, a contract was awarded to E. P. McGovern in 1893 to relocate the bodies from Mt. Prospect to Riverside. Being paid by the body, McGovern quickly found ways to increase his take by hacking up an adult body to fill three children's coffins. There was an investigation, and McGovern's contract was duly canceled. The Mt. Prospect Cemetery site was cleaned up, though it is estimated that 2,000 bodies remain under what later became Cheesman Park. To this day workers sometimes find bodies when digging irrigation lines. Lewis H. Musgrave may lie under Cheesman Park, or he may be buried in Riverside Cemetery, and he may even be in both.

For years after the Wild West had ceased to be any type of reality, its image was kept alive by people such as Buffalo Bill Cody, who entertained large crowds with his traveling performances around the United States and Europe. These extravaganzas had demonstrations of horsemanship and marksmanship by cowboys and Plains Indians and reenactments of military battles and hunts. This sensationalized and romanticized version of the West, ignoring the murder and exploitation of the Native Americans, was further embedded in the minds of the public by Western novels and Hollywood movies. A version of Lewis Musgrave's infamous exploits was depicted in the 1955 television series *Stories of the Century*, featuring a railroad detective who tracked down famous outlaws of the Wild West.[99] While there were cattle rustlers and gunslingers, lawmen and their posses, and occasions of mob justice, these incidents were relatively rare. Soon this short period in history came to an end as farms, ranches, and towns overtook the last frontier at a galloping pace.

15

The End of One Era and the Start of Another

———— • ————

The 1860s marked a period of transition for Napa Valley. The days of pioneers on the frontier were coming to an end. The large cattle ranches were becoming less viable, while the value of the land was increasing as more people moved into the area. With them came different ways of making a living, and in turn, new businesses and buildings sprung up throughout the countryside. One new industry in the valley was mining for silver and mercury, which was short-lived but brought a brief spurt of notoriety and miners to the region. By the end of the decade, a railroad ran through the upvalley towns, expanding all types of commerce. Frontier life was fading as the Victorian era speedily approached.

Hastening the end of large cattle ranches was the cattle depression beginning in the winter of 1861. Seventy straight days of rain brought fifty inches of rainfall and extreme flooding, resulting in hundreds of thousands of cattle drowning. As if that were not devastating enough, by the fall of 1862, the land had become bone dry, and a three-year drought starved many more animals. Unable to feed their cattle, ranchers sold them off, and due to the glut of animals for sale, prices dropped significantly. At this time, Henry Fowler was both a cattleman and money lender. Like everyone else, he lost cattle and had to sell the thin animals at a reduced rate. He also had to foreclose on properties, as even prominent people in the community became over-extended on their mortgages.

No history of the Upper Napa Valley would be complete without mention of Sam Brannan. In July 1846, Brannan led a group of Mormons by ship to San Francisco, and then he helped set up settlements for them. He brought with him mill machinery and a printing press, both of which enabled him to build a financial empire. In January of 1847, he started the first newspaper in San Francisco called the *California Star*. He also had a store at Sutter's Fort, which proved to be very profitable during the Gold Rush. It is said that Brannan stocked his store with every available good before announcing the discovery of gold in California. He opened other stores in the mining country, and the steep markups in prices made him the first millionaire in California. It is said that while Brannan was an elder of the Mormon Church, he neglected to send the tithes he received back to the main church, further adding to his coffers. In a relatively short time, Brannan had become a prominent man in San Francisco and Sacramento as both a land-owner and businessman.

Brannan first visited Napa Valley in 1852, staying at the exclusive White Sulphur Springs Resort near present-day St. Helena. He became enamored with the idea of running a resort and looked into the hot springs located further up the valley on the Fowler Ranch. Impressed by the springs' spectac-ular setting and abundant waters, he was convinced he could make it into a world-class spa.

Brannan often visited the Fowler Ranch, and in 1857 he bought the land around the hot springs. By that time, the land had changed hands a few times since the Fowlers first sold it, and Brannan bought it from Martha Ritchie.[100] Brannan neglected to pay the taxes on the land and lost it, but he bought it again in 1859.

By 1860, Brannan had built the two-story Hot Springs Hotel, and in 1862 he opened his new resort. His guests stayed in cottages and enjoyed various bathing pavilions set in a park-like atmosphere. These were the first of many buildings and embellishments he would add to the property over the years. Eventually, the resort would include a race track, stables, vineyards, a skating rink, a ballroom, and an observatory on the small hill called Mt. Lincoln next to the hot springs. In 1863, Brannan added to his 640 acres by buying 1,000 acres from the Fowler & Hargrave ranch. They struck a deal in which Brannan paid $1,200 for the land around his hot springs property from the river to the eastern hills, while Fowler & Hargrave received over 4,400 acres in nearby Knights Valley for $4,000.

CALISTOGA HOT SULPHUR SPRINGS.

Postcard of Early Calistoga

There are many versions of how Hot Springs came to be renamed Calistoga in 1865. The most common and interesting one is that Sam Brannan was describing his often-told plans to create a spa that would rival or better the spas of Europe and Saratoga Springs in New York. His speech was colored by the amount of alcohol he had drunk when he said, "I'm going to make it the Calistoga of Sarafornia!" Whether an accident or not, the name stuck.

Around the resort, Brannan proceeded to lay out the new town of Calistoga, along with a store, more vineyards, and a distillery. There were plans for a railroad depot, town hall, and even an exotic tea garden and mulberry orchard for raising silkworms. As grand as Brannan's plans were, he increasingly alienated some of the area's early settlers. For all the good he had brought to the town including his philanthropy, he was a problematic financial businessman who could be mean and selfish. He was so unpopular that at one point a man shot Brannan eight times over a financial dispute. Remarkably, Brannan survived with only partial paralysis in his hip.

While local controversy over the growth of the town continued, so did progress. The first train rolled into Calistoga in August of 1867, connecting the small resort town with the more populated areas to the south. In spite of

Brannan's uneven reputation, and likely because of constant pressure from him, Henry Fowler formed a brief partnership with Brannan. However, Henry soon found their relationship untenable, and he sold his share to Brannan in 1868. By this time, Sam Brannan's wife was also fed up with his shenanigans, and in their 1870 divorce court settlement, she won half of their community property, forcing Brannan to liquidate some of his investments. While Calistoga continued to prosper under new owners, this marked the beginning of the end for Brannan's financial success, and twenty years later he died a poor man.

After William Fowler's return from Hawaii, he resumed living on the Fowler Ranch. When Henry got married in 1857, he built a small home for his father near his own house, located on what is now the southeast corner of Lincoln and Myrtle Streets in the town of Calistoga. The Cottage, as it was called by the family, was a boarding house of sorts where some of the ranch labor also lived. Later, the building served as the first school in Calistoga, before a schoolhouse was built.

William Fowler continued to keep his rosewood coffin under his bed. Unknown to William, Henry's wife Catherine Magness Fowler found the lid of the coffin useful as an ironing board. William would have been offended by such a mundane use of his coffin, and so no one told him.

William always maintained close relationships with his family, even his former wife, Kitty, and her family. For many years, William would walk across the creek and valley to Kitty's home and share Sunday dinner with the family. Even in his older years when William suffered from cataracts, he would take his walking stick and stride down the path to her place on Sundays. One evening on his way home, he slipped crossing the creek and was unable to get up. The next morning, his grandson found William still lying there. The fall and the exposure were more than William could overcome, and the patriarch of the Fowler family died of pneumonia on February 3, 1865, at Henry's home. He was buried in the beautiful rosewood coffin that he had made for the occasion many years before. Where William Fowler was finally laid to rest was not recorded, though it is likely that he was interred in the cemetery next to the old White Church alongside his daughter Catherine and other early settlers.

William Fowler's life spanned eighty-five remarkable years. He was born during the Revolutionary War, ten years before George Washington became president, and he died during the Civil War, just a couple of months before

Abraham Lincoln was shot. He moved from Albany, New York across an expanding country all the way to the Pacific Coast, and eventually to the Hawaiian Islands. He traveled across the West in his sixties, and throughout his life he built dozens of buildings by hand, working well into his seventies. He likely never rode on a train or steamship, getting around mostly by horse and on foot. William lived his entire life on the frontier, and his death coincided with the end of an era.

William Fowler's obituary in the February 9, 1865, San Francisco *Daily Alta California* read:[101]

> *DEATH OF A PIONEER.*
> *Napa Valley, Feb. 4ᵗʰ, 1865.*
>
> *Editors Alta: William Fowler, Sr. one of the earliest pioneers of California, departed this life on the 3rd inst., at the residence of his son Henry, at Calistoga, Napa Valley. The deceased, having migrated with his children to Oregon as early as 1843, and having sojourned there sufficiently long to leave remarkable evidence of his skill as a builder, he proceeded to California, entertaining the conviction that here was a broad field for the development of agriculture and commerce. Early in 1844, he took up his residence in Napa Valley, purchasing, under the Mexican Government, a fertile tract of country, bounded by the pine-clad hills of the St. Helena range of mountains. Here he found a salubrious climate, and, to a great extent, the realization of his wishes. Surrounded by his children, and subsequently by many associates of his younger days, from his far Eastern home in Albany, N.Y., he concluded to spend the balance of his years in the quiet pursuit of husbandry. Having for many years aided and participated in every good project to advance the interests of his adopted State, and to his last days gave evidence of his stern and patriotic principles as a true American citizen, a good husbandman and exemplary father, he has, much lamented by all who knew him, taken his departure from among us, in the eighty-sixth year of his age.*
> *T. B. G.*

A little over a year later, tragedy struck the Fowler family again. At just under 36 years of age, Ann Eliza Fowler Harlan died on June 30, 1866, in San Leandro, Alameda County. There is no record of why Ann died, but it may have been due to complications from childbirth. Her last two children had died within months of being born, and Ann died after bearing another child, who also died within months. The local paper noted that Ann's funeral was one of the biggest the town of San Leandro had seen. She had grown up on the frontier and celebrated her sixteenth birthday on the trail to California. She raised her family and dealt with the ups and downs of her husband's various business ventures. Six of her nine children survived her, ranging in age from 6 to 18 years old.

Ann's husband, Jacob Harlan, was devastated and never really thrived after her death. In the late 1850s, he and Ann had moved to San Leandro, and for a while, Jacob was quite prosperous. He owned seventy-five acres in a triangle between East 14th Street, Washington Avenue, and San Leandro Boulevard. A street there still bears his name. Following Ann's death, he continued to live with his children in San Leandro for six more years. In 1872, he sold his properties and moved up to Calistoga to try running a hotel, but he was not suited

Jacob Wright Harlan

to it. In 1873, he went to work on a farm near Livermore. After saving up some money, Jacob bought land north of Livermore, where he lived for a few years. He continued to move around, and in his last few years, he returned to San Leandro. In 1888, Jacob Harlan published reminiscences of his life in a book titled *California '46 to '86*. While it is valuable for its description of his experiences coming west and of his life while married to Ann Fowler, as with most memoirs, it is also colored by Jacob's desire to be remembered in a favorable light. Jacob would live for several more decades, but he would never achieve the stature or well-being he had while married to Ann Fowler.

By the late 1860s, Henry Fowler was ready to move out of Calistoga for numerous reasons. Ever since the Gold Rush, Henry had been dealing with squatters on his land, and he was tired of defending his property against their claims. His partnership with Sam Brannan, one of Calistoga's biggest movers and shakers, had not worked out. Finally, there were considerations for his family, specifically the education of his three school-age daughters. They had been attending the first school in Calistoga, but the town of Napa had better and more established schools. In 1868, Henry Fowler and his partner William Hargrave sold their remaining Calistoga ranch lands to Sam Brannan for $4,500 and moved their families to Napa twenty-five miles south of Calistoga.

The Napa River flows through broad marshlands as it meanders northwards from the San Francisco Bay, and the town of Napa was built at the point where the navigable portion of the river ends. Like the neighboring town of Sonoma, Napa sits at the base of a long valley that stretches north into the coastal mountains. General Vallejo's brother Salvador Vallejo was given a land grant for the area in 1838, but it was another ten years before the town took shape.

Henry Fowler moved with his wife and five children to a home on the north corner of Clay and Franklin Streets in downtown Napa, now 1340 Clay Street. Catherine Magness Fowler's older unmarried sister, Mary, lived with them full time, as was customary at the time. Generally, an extra pair of female hands was welcomed to help with the running of a household and looking after children, and there were few options for women to live on their own. Catherine's other siblings and Henry's brother Bill would also stay with them from time to time. Like her sister-in-law Minerva, Catherine prided herself on her Southern hospitality and her ability to cook up a feast for guests and family alike. To help her in the kitchen, she employed Ah Tong, a live-in Chinese cook, a practice which was not unusual for those who could afford it.

Next door to the Fowlers, at 28 Franklin Street, was the Presbyterian Chinese Chapel. The chapel's Chinese mission offered English language classes and taught the principles of Christianity. It served as a cultural and social center for the local Chinese, and the largest holiday, Chinese Lunar

New Year, was celebrated at the mission until 1897. The number of Chinese men in California was sizable. Many came during the Gold Rush seeking their fortune, and afterward, they settled throughout the state, congregating in small communities near work opportunities. Due to significant social and legal discrimination, the types of employment open to the Chinese were limited. They found jobs as railroad workers, miners, farm labor, day labor, launderers, servants, and cooks. Napa Valley had a brief mining boom in the 1860s, which brought many Chinese men to the valley. Napa's Chinatown started at this time and reached its peak in the late 1800s with a population of about nine hundred. It was located on First Street, at the confluence of Napa Creek and the Napa River, just four blocks from Henry's home.

By 1870, Henry had transitioned from ranching to money lending and real estate. Besides two hundred acres of land at the north end of Main Street, Henry also became a partner in the East Napa Land Company with four other men.[102] The company owned and developed land all along the east side of the Napa River. He was also a Trustee for the Napa Collegiate Institute, one of the earliest institutions of higher learning in the region. His daughters were enrolled at the Institute where they studied music, drawing, painting, and elocution.

Henry Fowler was becoming a wealthy, prominent, and respected citizen in his newly adopted home. When Napa was incorporated as a town in 1872, Henry Fowler was selected as one of the five original members of the Board of Trustees. In 1875, Henry and his partners in the East Napa Land Company built the Palace Hotel on Third Street just across the bridge from downtown. It was an impressive three-story building and the fanciest hotel in town.

Just as William Fowler's death coincided with the end of an era, Henry's move off the ranch and into the town of Napa was emblematic of his stepping into a new one. The town of Napa had electricity and gas service, a telegraph line, and both train and steamboat connections to other San Francisco Bay Area towns.

By 1870, a new era was dawning, one built on the shoulders of the preceding period. For example, the first local railroads appeared in California in the mid-1850s, but, by 1870, a full Atlantic to Pacific rail crossing of the United States was possible. The route the transcontinental railroad took largely followed the old California Trail. It went through Weber Canyon to cross the Wasatch Mountains in Utah, the same hard-won path taken by the Harlan Party, the Fowlers, and many of the Upper Napa Valley families who came west in 1846. To traverse the steep canyon, the railroad required the construction of bridges and four long tunnels, dangerous work for the largely Mormon crew who built it. The train also traveled through Donner Pass across the Sierra Nevada Mountains. The last connection the railroad needed to reach the San Francisco Bay was made just upstream from where Jacob Harlan had his ferry ten years before with the construction of the San Joaquin River Bridge at Mossdale Crossing.

The transcontinental railroad cut the time it took to cross the country from months to days, and so the east and west portions of the country were joined together, with trade and people crisscrossing the continent as never before. While the frontier would continue in the Mountain States for twenty-five more years, that way of life mostly disappeared in California as the state entered a period of even more rapid growth.

Palace Hotel, Napa City

16

The Passing of the Last Pioneers

———— • ————

The Fowler family had suffered from the death of loved ones as they traveled across the frontier and settled in California, but compared to many, they had been fortunate in their ability to survive so many challenges. Starting in the 1870s, however, death cast its shadow over the family more frequently as illness and age took their toll.[103]

After a long and painful illness, Minerva's husband, Joel Harlan, died of stomach cancer on March 28, 1875, at the age of 46. Joel had worked with his cousin Jacob Harlan on many enterprises early on, and in his later years, he had become a skilled financier and a major landowner in Contra Costa County with an estate of 2,000 acres. Joel Harlan also helped the needy in his community and supported the development of educational opportunities in the region. He was described as "popular and esteemed," "upright and genial," and "greatly respected and much beloved, not only by his own family and relatives but also by the citizens of the county."[104]

Kitty Speed Fowler Musgrave spent sixty years living on the frontier, much of that time raising children, her own as well as those of her daughter, Catherine. In Calistoga, Kitty and her family were part of the early upvalley community, many of whom had made the overland journey to California with her in 1846. Over the years, the community had grown from a handful of families into a town and resort. Kitty spent thirty years on the Calistoga ranch, the longest she had lived anywhere. As is unfortunately true for most women in history, accounts of her life and activities are few and far between. Relatively little is known about Kitty's daily life other than through inference based on the events that happened around her. One small particular that comes from Fowler Mallet is that her eyes were very sensitive to light, a quality her son Henry also inherited. This meant that she often had to shade her eyes even when indoors. This tiny detail is just a small indication of the persevering nature she had. While visiting her son Henry Fowler and his family in Napa, Kitty, the matriarch of the Fowler Family, died on May 22, 1876, at the age of 74. Her final resting place is marked by an impressive headstone in Tulocay Cemetery in Napa, not far from the markers for her son Henry and his family. Kitty's husband,

Kitty's Gravestone in Napa

Calvin Musgrave, continued to live in Calistoga, though he was the last of the extended Fowler family to call Calistoga home.

It was Calvin who provided the last home for Peter Storm, a long-time friend of the family. Storm died at the Fowler Ranch on December 14, 1877. He had often worked and lived with the Fowlers as well as other Upper Napa Valley residents, especially the Cyrus family. Elizabeth Cyrus Wright remembered her brothers saying that, after drinking a bit of alcohol, Storm would recount wild and wonderful pirate stories. By the time Peter Storm reached the ripe old age of 78, he had many more tales to tell about his experiences as one of the earliest Euro-Americans in the Napa Valley as well. He was a beloved character in the community and was "Uncle Peter" to everyone who knew him. He was most renowned for creating one of the first California flags and would proudly march with his flag in parades decades after the Bear Flag Revolt. It is said he was even buried with his flag, or possibly a replica he made years later.

In the U.S. census conducted on June 30, 1880, Calvin Musgrave, then widowed, is shown living in the county hospital in Santa Rosa, listed as paralyzed and mentally diminished resulting from a stroke or accident. It also says that he had been unemployed for at least the previous twelve months. Four years after his wife Kitty's death, and still in Santa Rosa, Calvin Musgrave died on October 9, 1880, at the age of 60.

The Fowler & Hargrave ranch in Calistoga had been the home base for the Fowler family from the time of their arrival in California in the 1840s. With Calvin Musgrave's move to the hospital in Santa Rosa in 1879, there ceased to be any members of the Fowler clan living in Calistoga. They had worked and lived in the Upper Napa Valley for thirty-four years, from 1845 to 1879, participating in the growth of the region from a remote outpost to prosperous ranches, and eventually, a Victorian town. Over time, the family and its descendants had moved on and were living throughout the greater San Francisco Bay Area, from the town of Napa in the north to Contra Costa County in the south.

The famed California historian Hubert Howe Bancroft recorded the names of ninety-six men who arrived in California in 1844 and stayed as foreign residents. Bancroft noted that about twenty of those ninety-six men were still alive in 1884. He interviewed many of them, including Henry Fowler and William Hargrave, to record early California history from those who had lived it. By 1898, fifty years after the discovery of gold, the local Napa newspapers listed thirty-five men who had come to California before the Gold Rush and who were still living in Napa County. Henry and Bill Fowler were listed among them.

Bill Fowler, the oldest of the Fowler siblings, had been living with either Henry or Minerva for almost fifty years after the accident that left him permanently impaired. It was at Minerva's home near San Ramon that Bill made his final journey on January 15, 1901. He was 83 years old. Bill had been born in Albany, New York, and had moved west with the family. Despite his formal education, Bill's true love was traveling throughout the frontier. Bill made five trips between Missouri and the West in the 1840s and was one of the first emigrants traveling some of the earliest trails. He was a true trailblazer.

Bill was survived by his son, William Henry Fowler III. Fowler Mallett described William as embodying Bill's adventurous spirit and also sharing his passion for mining. William prospected in Idaho and later, lived for many years near the Oregon border in Happy Camp, California, named for the area's early mining prosperity. Married for a short time, William and his wife had two children. William Henry Fowler III died in 1926.[105]

During Jacob Harlan's later years, he struggled with both alcohol and poverty. His issues with excessive drinking appeared in the local newspapers, and he occasionally lived in veterans homes, including the state veterans home in Yountville, Napa Valley. At times, he appeared to be destitute except for a small Army Pension for his service in the Mexican-American War. At the age of 66, Jacob married a woman named Christina McDonald, and hopefully, that brought him some contentment in his last years. On March 7, 1902, Jacob Harlan died in San Leandro at the age of 73. From the tales he told of his life, Jacob was quick to try new things and to take risks which led to a colorful life. Over the years, he worked in a wide array of professions as a soldier, lumberman, livery stable owner, dairyman, storekeeper, ferryman, landowner, rancher, farmer, and hotelier. As his story reveals, the lives of pioneers were not simply ones of either success or failure, and many people had several careers, making and losing fortunes along the way. Jacob Harlan is an example of someone who died financially impoverished after a hard-working and memorable life. This pattern was not uncommon at the time and can be observed in the lives of some of the more famous Californians, such as Sam Brannan, John Sutter, John Fremont, and Mariano Vallejo.

Henry Fowler enjoyed the ease and comforts of his later years, after his more adventurous and hard-working youth. Henry's grandson, Fowler Mallett, recalled the family joking that Henry had not done a lick of work since turning 40. This was an exaggeration, of course. Henry Fowler managed the Palace Hotel from 1888 to 1897 and was joined by his son-in-law Sherwood Bird from 1894 until they sold the hotel in 1900.[106] In his personal time, Henry took pride in keeping his home running smoothly, and he was an avid gardener as well.

Henry was very fond of his children, and Fowler Mallett speculates that he may have indulged them in reaction to his own father's austere attitude toward Henry and his siblings. Whatever the reason, by this time in his life, Henry had the means and the time to be a doting father and husband. He was said to have a gentle voice, and he only raised it during rare moments of exasperation.

As a result of his early contributions to the railroad, Henry and his family had lifetime passes to ride between Napa and San Francisco. This access to San Francisco delighted his stylish wife and teenage daughters, who were frequent customers at San Francisco's luxury stores, such as The White House, City of Paris, Davis Schonwasser, and O'Connor & Moffatt. Meanwhile, Henry went to San Francisco for business and to visit friends. He also attended meetings of the Society of California Pioneers, founded in 1850 and was made up of those who had come to California before statehood.

William Hargrave and Henry Fowler were longtime friends whose lives had run in parallel from the time they were young men. Later, their daughters were such close friends that they considered themselves cousins, and generally, the two families felt themselves to be part of one great family. As older men living in Napa, William and Henry were able to sustain their friendship. This must have been a particular comfort after William lost his wife in 1873.[107] However, by the late 1880s, William's health was failing, and in his last few years, he became an invalid. On September 21, 1890, William Hargrave died at the age of 72. He was survived by five children as well as by his good friend Henry Fowler.

Henry's daughters had moved from Napa to San Francisco, and in 1892, they convinced Henry and his wife to give big city living a try.[108] It is easy to imagine the lively and social Catherine Magness Fowler taking to city life, but, in the case of Henry, he soon realized that all the hustle and bustle was not to his liking. At the end of the year, he and his wife returned to Napa, where Henry would live out his days.

Henry Fowler lost his sight in his last year due to cataracts. Forced to stay at his home in Napa, he became weaker and finally succumbed to an illness on October 18, 1904. He was 82 years old. His funeral was led by the Masonic Order, and it was one of the largest ever in Napa, with people coming from far and wide to honor him. He was well known and perhaps equally important, well-liked, and many took the occasion to write glowing tributes to him.

The *San Francisco Call* wrote:[109]

Probably no man in Northern California was better known or more universally beloved than Henry Fowler.

He was strongly identified with the early history of Napa County and was interested in many of her enterprises. He was a man of pure character and strong intellect and was widely known for his many kindly acts.

William M. Boggs, the son of Governor Lillian Boggs and contemporary of Henry Fowler, opined:[110]

I have lived a neighbor to Mr. Henry Fowler ... and knew him most intimately for fifty-seven years, and I can say with all truth and sincerity, that I never knew a more kindhearted and genial gentleman in all my acquaintance. ... No man in Napa County and Sacramento County was better known than the late Henry Fowler. He was respected, and beloved by all who knew him, and particularly by his old pioneer friends, of whom I claim to be one of the first to know him in California.

Henry Fowler

Henry Fowler had come to California and lived in Napa Valley for sixty years. He had been a frontier carpenter, cattle rancher, gold miner, and capitalist. Unlike many in early California, Henry was able to accumulate and hold on to his wealth, enjoying the ease and comfort it afforded him in his old age. While his skill and prudence helped him to make a fortune, keeping it was a result of his personable and steady character, along with some luck. Henry has not been remembered by history as prominently as other famous California characters like Fremont, Brannan, and Vallejo, but he worked with them, and in the end, he was considered to have played an important role in the development of Calistoga and Napa.

Henry was survived by his wife, Catherine Magness Fowler, and all four of their daughters. Catherine was known for her generosity, directness, and her youthful demeanor. She displayed a zest for living throughout her life, even taking tango lessons in her later years. She also served as the family archivist and kept three volumes of newspaper clippings about the Fowlers and their relations. Those records were helpful to people like her grandson, Fowler Mallett, who later wrote a history of the family.[111]

An hour before dawn on the morning of April 18, 1906, while most people were still in bed, there was a loud rumbling followed by thirty seconds of shaking. This was just the beginning of a nightmare for the citizens of San Francisco and nearby towns. Twenty seconds later, another shock hit, this time lasting forty seconds and creating one of the biggest natural disasters in the history of the United States. The earthquake had a magnitude of 7.9, and it was felt as far away as Los Angeles and Oregon.

Though the quake was over in minutes, the resulting fires caused much of the subsequent destruction of San Francisco. The city burned for four days, and by the end, four square miles, 500 city blocks, 28,000 buildings, and eighty percent of San Francisco was leveled.

The devastation was described by Jerome Clark, who had arrived that morning on the ferry:[112]

> In every direction from the ferry building flames were seething, and as I stood there, a five-story building half a block away fell with a crash, and the flames swept clear across Market Street and caught a new fireproof building recently erected. The streets in places had sunk three or four feet, in others great humps had appeared four or five feet high. The street car tracks were bent and twisted out

*of shape. Electric wires lay in every direction. Streets on all
sides were filled with brick and mortar, buildings either
completely collapsed or brick fronts had just dropped completely off. Wagons with horses hitched to them, drivers
and all, lying on the streets, all dead, struck and killed by
the falling bricks.*

Throughout the ordeal, 3,000 people died, and almost 300,000 of the
400,000 people of San Francisco were left homeless. Some were still living
in refugee camps two years later.

From north to south, towns throughout the greater San Francisco Bay
Area experienced significant destruction and suffered many deaths. Seventy-
five miles away, the mouth of the Salinas River shifted six miles to the south.
In Marin County, just north of San Francisco, a steam locomotive was
knocked over as the land moved by as much as twenty feet.

San Francisco had grown rapidly following the Gold Rush and not
always in an orderly fashion. The opportunity to rebuild the city almost
from scratch would ultimately result in it becoming a much bigger and
better city than before. In the meantime, many neighboring cities like
Oakland and San Jose were built up as people and businesses relocated to
these less damaged communities. While San Francisco eventually rose from
the ashes, the setback allowed Los Angeles to supersede it and become the
largest urban area on the West Coast.

Minerva Fowler Harlan was the only Fowler sibling living during the
1906 earthquake. Minerva and her husband, Joel, had created a large and
loving home, raising an abandoned Native American child and four other
children they had taken in, alongside their own eight offspring. She had lost
her husband Joel Harlan in 1875, and five of their children did not live to
see 1900.

Having grieved so many loved ones, Minerva came to believe in the
ability to communicate with the dead using a wooden planchette, through
which she would receive messages from departed family members. This
method of talking to the dead had become popular with the advent of
various spiritualist movements of the time. The messages Minerva received
were usually positive and consoled her with the sense that those who had
passed on were in a better place. Given this reassurance, no one in the
family had the heart to dispute the phenomenon.

Minerva Fowler Harlan

Minerva also had the consolation of the comfortable home and garden that she and her husband had built up over the years at *Rancho El Nido* near San Ramon in Contra Costa County. She was part of a large extended family that included her five surviving children and their families, and she had her musical, artistic, and domestic pursuits as well. She is said to have been healthy right up until the time when she passed away in her sleep on March 24, 1915, at the home of her daughter in Oakland. She was 82 years old and the last of the Fowler siblings. Within the extended family, she was survived by only two other women of her generation.

Of course, the Fowler family lived on. Twenty of the thirty-five grand-children were still alive in 1915, as well as forty-two great-grandchildren. One of those grandchildren was Ella Musgrave, the daughter of Catherine Fowler and Lewis Musgrave. She was born in Hot Springs, present-day Calistoga, in 1857 and was raised there by her grandmother Kitty on the Fowler Ranch. Ella is the author's grandmother's grandmother and was the inspiration for this book.

Ella Musgrave

Conclusion

———————— • ————————

The Fowlers were one family of many who experienced the challenges and rewards of life in early California. While a few dozen people are generally highlighted in the telling of California's history in the 1840s, thousands more had a part in shaping those times. Most of them were ranchers and miners, housewives and shopkeepers, tradesmen and laborers. Their stories are often not recorded, especially the stories of the women.

To survive, each pioneer needed a diverse set of skills to meet the demands of frontier life and to navigate the ups and downs of their daily lives. The men often had multiple careers, which they adopted for any number of reasons. Sometimes there would be a sudden change in the resources or economies around them as drought struck, cattle prices plummeted, or gold was discovered. Similarly, they might face a shift in the needs of their family as loved ones died and new ones were born. The women had to be equally adaptive and persevering as they sought to keep their family fed, clean, healthy, and clothed with limited resources. Children often took on responsibilities at a very early age, helping with chores, looking after the animals, and caring for the younger children. Everyone dealt with the hardships of life, contending with disease and death, accidents, and plain old hard work.

Along with the difficulties, the pioneers also experienced many of the good things in life: the strong support of family and community, a sense of accomplishment in overcoming great obstacles, new opportunities, as well as the more fundamental joys of falling in love, the birth of a child, or even the satisfaction of a hearty meal. These moments are usually lost to history, but they inevitably made up the texture of daily life then as they do now.

While history is often told by an accounting of exceptional events and people, our past is primarily the result of the daily lives of countless people doing all the things that people do. The story of the Fowlers offers yet one more glimpse of what life was like for some of the folks who set out to explore and live in the West during a dynamic time in U.S. history. Like the Fowlers, each family's story is unique and adds to our understanding of who we were and offers a perspective on who we are today.

FOWLER
Family Tree

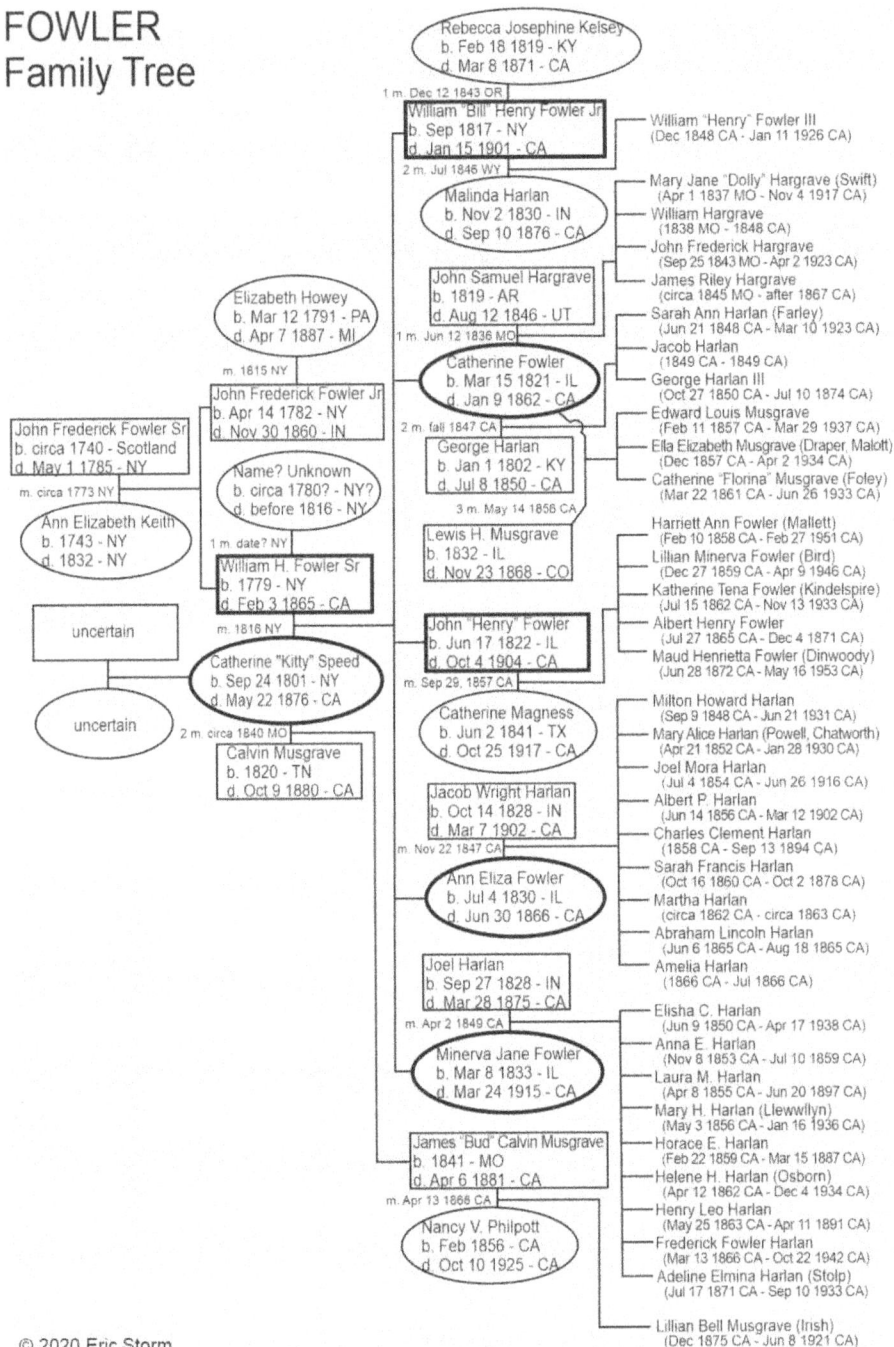

Rebecca Josephine Kelsey
b. Feb 18 1819 - KY
d. Mar 8 1871 - CA

1 m. Dec 12 1843 OR

William "Bill" Henry Fowler Jr
b. Sep 1817 - NY
d. Jan 15 1901 - CA

William "Henry" Fowler III
(Dec 1848 CA - Jan 11 1926 CA)

2 m. Jul 1846 WY

Malinda Harlan
b. Nov 2 1830 - IN
d. Sep 10 1876 - CA

Mary Jane "Dolly" Hargrave (Swift)
(Apr 1 1837 MO - Nov 4 1917 CA)

William Hargrave
(1838 MO - 1848 CA)

John Frederick Hargrave
(Sep 25 1843 MO - Apr 2 1923 CA)

John Samuel Hargrave
b. 1819 - AR
d. Aug 12 1846 - UT

James Riley Hargrave
(circa 1845 MO - after 1867 CA)

1 m. Jun 12 1836 MO

Sarah Ann Harlan (Farley)
(Jun 21 1848 CA - Mar 10 1923 CA)

Jacob Harlan
(1849 CA - 1849 CA)

Elizabeth Howey
b. Mar 12 1791 - PA
d. Apr 7 1887 - MI

Catherine Fowler
b. Mar 15 1821 - IL
d. Jan 9 1862 - CA

George Harlan III
(Oct 27 1850 CA - Jul 10 1874 CA)

m. 1815 NY

2 m. fall 1847 CA

Edward Louis Musgrave
(Feb 11 1857 CA - Mar 29 1937 CA)

John Frederick Fowler Jr
b. Apr 14 1782 - NY
d. Nov 30 1860 - IN

George Harlan
b. Jan 1 1802 - KY
d. Jul 8 1850 - CA

Ella Elizabeth Musgrave (Draper, Malott)
(Dec 1857 CA - Apr 2 1934 CA)

John Frederick Fowler Sr
b. circa 1740 - Scotland
d. May 1 1785 - NY

Catherine "Florina" Musgrave (Foley)
(Mar 22 1861 CA - Jun 26 1933 CA)

3 m. May 14 1856 CA

m. circa 1773 NY

Name? Unknown
b. circa 1780? - NY?
d. before 1816 - NY

Lewis H. Musgrave
b. 1832 - IL
d. Nov 23 1868 - CO

Harriett Ann Fowler (Mallett)
(Feb 10 1858 CA - Feb 27 1951 CA)

Ann Elizabeth Keith
b. 1743 - NY
d. 1832 - NY

Lillian Minerva Fowler (Bird)
(Dec 27 1859 CA - Apr 9 1946 CA)

1 m. date? NY

Katherine Tena Fowler (Kindelspire)
(Jul 15 1862 CA - Nov 13 1933 CA)

William H. Fowler Sr
b. 1779 - NY
d. Feb 3 1865 - CA

John "Henry" Fowler
b. Jun 17 1822 - IL
d. Oct 4 1904 - CA

Albert Henry Fowler
(Jul 27 1865 CA - Dec 4 1871 CA)

uncertain

m. 1818 NY

Maud Henrietta Fowler (Dinwoody)
(Jun 28 1872 CA - May 16 1953 CA)

m. Sep 29, 1857 CA

Catherine "Kitty" Speed
b. Sep 24 1801 - NY
d. May 22 1876 - CA

Catherine Magness
b. Jun 2 1841 - TX
d. Oct 25 1917 - CA

Milton Howard Harlan
(Sep 9 1848 CA - Jun 21 1931 CA)

uncertain

Mary Alice Harlan (Powell, Chatworth)
(Apr 21 1852 CA - Jan 28 1930 CA)

2 m. circa 1840 MO

Joel Mora Harlan
(Jul 4 1854 CA - Jun 26 1916 CA)

Calvin Musgrave
b. 1820 - TN
d. Oct 9 1880 - CA

Jacob Wright Harlan
b. Oct 14 1828 - IN
d. Mar 7 1902 - CA

Albert P. Harlan
(Jun 14 1856 CA - Mar 12 1902 CA)

Charles Clement Harlan
(1858 CA - Sep 13 1894 CA)

m. Nov 22 1847 CA

Sarah Francis Harlan
(Oct 16 1860 CA - Oct 2 1878 CA)

Ann Eliza Fowler
b. Jul 4 1830 - IL
d. Jun 30 1866 - CA

Martha Harlan
(circa 1862 CA - circa 1863 CA)

Abraham Lincoln Harlan
(Jun 6 1865 CA - Aug 18 1865 CA)

Joel Harlan
b. Sep 27 1828 - IN
d. Mar 28 1875 - CA

Amelia Harlan
(1866 CA - Jul 1866 CA)

m. Apr 2 1849 CA

Elisha C. Harlan
(Jun 9 1850 CA - Apr 17 1938 CA)

Anna E. Harlan
(Nov 8 1853 CA - Jul 10 1859 CA)

Minerva Jane Fowler
b. Mar 8 1833 - IL
d. Mar 24 1915 - CA

Laura M. Harlan
(Apr 8 1855 CA - Jun 20 1897 CA)

Mary H. Harlan (Llewwllyn)
(May 3 1856 CA - Jan 16 1936 CA)

Horace E. Harlan
(Feb 22 1859 CA - Mar 15 1887 CA)

James "Bud" Calvin Musgrave
b. 1841 - MO
d. Apr 6 1881 - CA

Helene H. Harlan (Osborn)
(Apr 12 1862 CA - Dec 4 1934 CA)

Henry Leo Harlan
(May 25 1863 CA - Apr 11 1891 CA)

m. Apr 13 1866 CA

Frederick Fowler Harlan
(Mar 13 1866 CA - Oct 22 1942 CA)

Nancy V. Philpott
b. Feb 1856 - CA
d. Oct 10 1925 - CA

Adeline Elmina Harlan (Stolp)
(Jul 17 1871 CA - Sep 10 1933 CA)

Lillian Bell Musgrave (Irish)
(Dec 1875 CA - Jun 8 1921 CA)

HARLAN
Family Tree

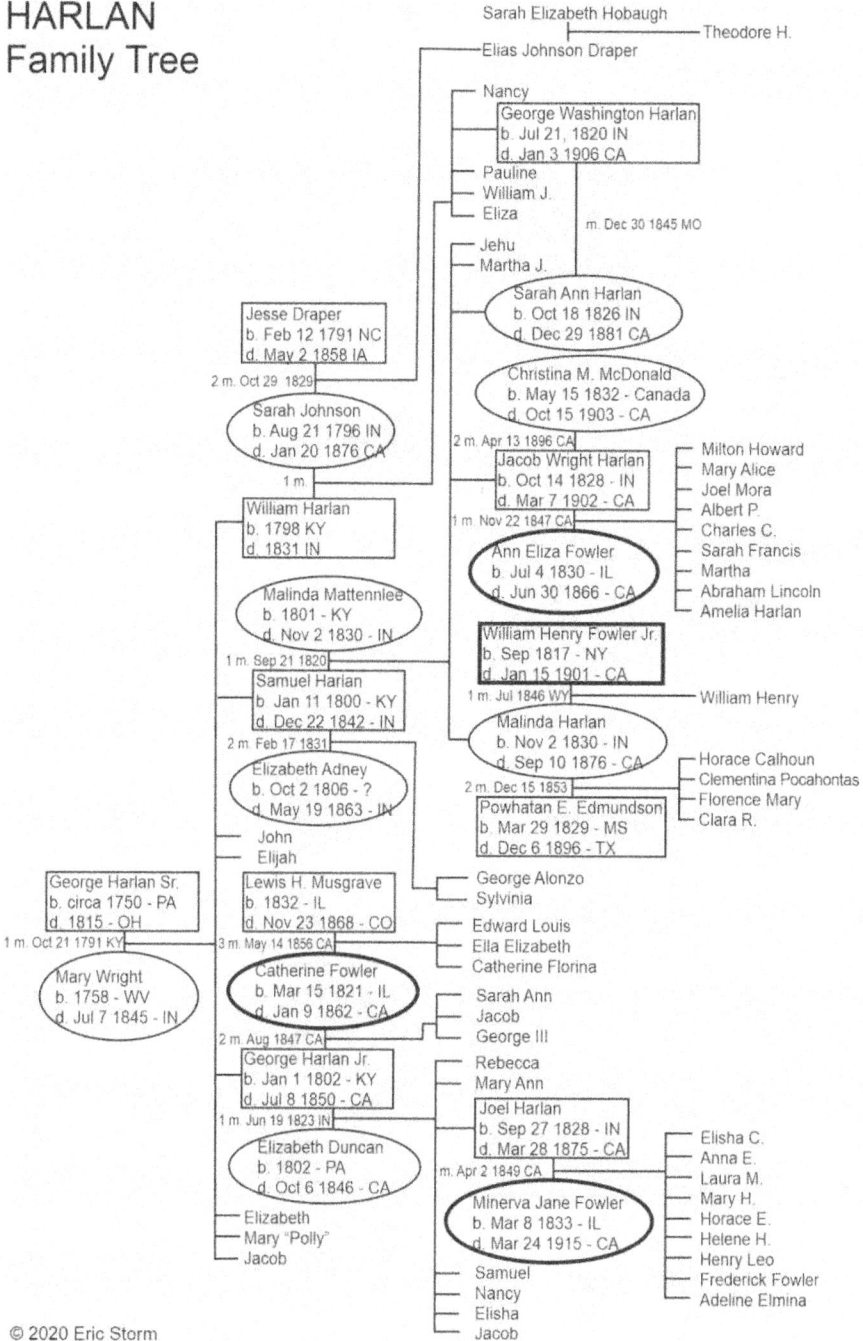

Sarah Elizabeth Hobaugh ──── Theodore H.

Elias Johnson Draper

Nancy

George Washington Harlan
b. Jul 21, 1820 IN
d. Jan 3 1906 CA

Pauline
William J.
Eliza

m. Dec 30 1845 MO

Jehu
Martha J.

Jesse Draper
b. Feb 12 1791 NC
d. May 2 1858 IA

Sarah Ann Harlan
b. Oct 18 1826 IN
d. Dec 29 1881 CA

2 m. Oct 29 1829

Christina M. McDonald
b. May 15 1832 - Canada
d. Oct 15 1903 - CA

Sarah Johnson
b. Aug 21 1796 IN
d. Jan 20 1876 CA

2 m. Apr 13 1896 CA

Jacob Wright Harlan
b. Oct 14 1828 - IN
d. Mar 7 1902 - CA

1 m.

William Harlan
b. 1798 KY
d. 1831 IN

1 m. Nov 22 1847 CA

Ann Eliza Fowler
b. Jul 4 1830 - IL
d. Jun 30 1866 - CA

Milton Howard
Mary Alice
Joel Mora
Albert P.
Charles C.
Sarah Francis
Martha
Abraham Lincoln
Amelia Harlan

Malinda Mattenniee
b. 1801 - KY
d. Nov 2 1830 - IN

1 m. Sep 21 1820

William Henry Fowler Jr.
b. Sep 1817 - NY
d. Jan 15 1901 - CA

Samuel Harlan
b. Jan 11 1800 - KY
d. Dec 22 1842 - IN

1 m. Jul 1846 WY

William Henry

Malinda Harlan
b. Nov 2 1830 - IN
d. Sep 10 1876 - CA

2 m. Feb 17 1831

Elizabeth Adney
b. Oct 2 1806 - ?
d. May 19 1863 - IN

2 m. Dec 15 1853

Powhatan E. Edmundson
b. Mar 29 1829 - MS
d. Dec 6 1896 - TX

Horace Calhoun
Clementina Pocahontas
Florence Mary
Clara R.

John
Elijah

George Harlan Sr.
b. circa 1750 - PA
d. 1815 - OH

Lewis H. Musgrave
b. 1832 - IL
d. Nov 23 1868 - CO

George Alonzo
Sylvinia

1 m. Oct 21 1791 KY

3 m. May 14 1856 CA

Edward Louis
Ella Elizabeth
Catherine Florina

Catherine Fowler
b. Mar 15 1821 - IL
d. Jan 9 1862 - CA

Mary Wright
b. 1758 - WV
d. Jul 7 1845 - IN

Sarah Ann
Jacob
George III

2 m. Aug 1847 CA

George Harlan Jr.
b. Jan 1 1802 - KY
d. Jul 8 1850 - CA

Rebecca
Mary Ann

Joel Harlan
b. Sep 27 1828 - IN
d. Mar 28 1875 - CA

1 m. Jun 19 1823 IN

m. Apr 2 1849 CA

Elisha C.
Anna E.
Laura M.
Mary H.
Horace E.
Helene H.
Henry Leo
Frederick Fowler
Adeline Elmina

Elizabeth Duncan
b. 1802 - PA
d. Oct 6 1846 - CA

Minerva Jane Fowler
b. Mar 8 1833 - IL
d. Mar 24 1915 - CA

Elizabeth
Mary "Polly"
Jacob

Samuel
Nancy
Elisha
Jacob

MUSGRAVE
Family Tree

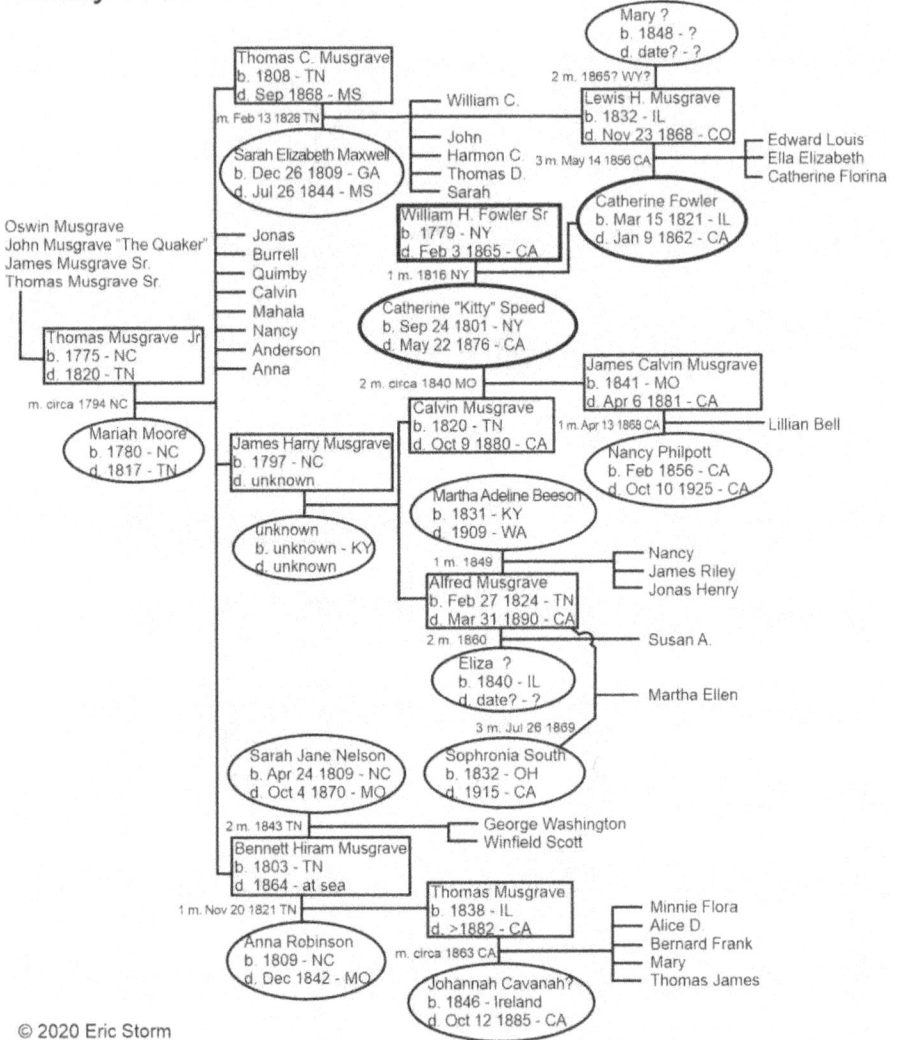

Mary ?
b. 1848 - ?
d. date? - ?

2 m. 1865? WY?

Thomas C. Musgrave
b. 1808 - TN
d. Sep 1868 - MS

m. Feb 13 1828 TN

William C.

Lewis H. Musgrave
b. 1832 - IL
d. Nov 23 1868 - CO

Edward Louis
Ella Elizabeth
Catherine Florina

John
Harmon C.   3 m. May 14 1856 CA
Thomas D.
Sarah

Sarah Elizabeth Maxwell
b. Dec 26 1809 - GA
d. Jul 26 1844 - MS

Catherine Fowler
b. Mar 15 1821 - IL
d. Jan 9 1862 - CA

William H. Fowler Sr
b. 1779 - NY
d. Feb 3 1865 - CA

Oswin Musgrave
John Musgrave "The Quaker"
James Musgrave Sr.
Thomas Musgrave Sr.

Jonas
Burrell
Quimby
Calvin
Mahala
Nancy
Anderson
Anna

1 m. 1816 NY

Catherine "Kitty" Speed
b. Sep 24 1801 - NY
d. May 22 1876 - CA

Thomas Musgrave Jr
b. 1775 - NC
d. 1820 - TN

James Calvin Musgrave
b. 1841 - MO
d. Apr 6 1881 - CA

2 m. circa 1840 MO

Calvin Musgrave
b. 1820 - TN
d. Oct 9 1880 - CA

1 m. Apr 13 1868 CA   Lillian Bell

m. circa 1794 NC

Mariah Moore
b. 1780 - NC
d. 1817 - TN

James Harry Musgrave
b. 1797 - NC
d. unknown

Nancy Philpott
b. Feb 1856 - CA
d. Oct 10 1925 - CA

Martha Adeline Beeson
b. 1831 - KY
d. 1909 - WA

unknown
b. unknown - KY
d. unknown

1 m. 1849

Nancy
James Riley
Jonas Henry

Alfred Musgrave
b. Feb 27 1824 - TN
d. Mar 31 1890 - CA

2 m. 1860   Susan A.

Eliza ?
b. 1840 - IL
d. date? - ?

Martha Ellen

3 m. Jul 26 1869

Sarah Jane Nelson
b. Apr 24 1809 - NC
d. Oct 4 1870 - MO

Sophronia South
b. 1832 - OH
d. 1915 - CA

2 m. 1843 TN

George Washington
Winfield Scott

Bennett Hiram Musgrave
b. 1803 - TN
d. 1864 - at sea

Thomas Musgrave
b. 1838 - IL
d. >1882 - CA

Minnie Flora
Alice D
Bernard Frank
Mary
Thomas James

1 m. Nov 20 1821 TN

m. circa 1863 CA

Anna Robinson
b. 1809 - NC
d. Dec 1842 - MO

Johannah Cavanah?
b. 1846 - Ireland
d. Oct 12 1885 - CA

References and Endnotes

General References (Selected references are listed under each chapter.)

Fowler, Henry. "How I Helped To Raise The Old Bear Flag." *The San Francisco Call*, January 23, 1898. 13:6.

——. *Raising Stock in Napa Valley*. January 17, 1886. Unpublished Manuscript of dictation recorded for H.H. Bancroft. Original at The Bancroft Library, University of California, Berkeley. BANC MSS C-D 260.

Guinn, James Miller. *History of the State of California and Biographical Record of Coast Counties, California. An Historical Story of the State's Marvelous Growth from its Earliest Settlement to the Present Time. Volumes I and II*. Chicago, IL: The Chapman Publishing Company, 1904.

Harlan, Jacob Wright. *California '46 to '88*. San Francisco, CA: The Bancroft Company, 1888.

Johnson, Overton, and William H. Winter. *Route Across the Rocky Mountains with a Description of Oregon and California, Etc., 1843*. Fairfield, WA: Ye Galleon Press, 1846.

Mallett, Fowler. *Genealogical Notes and Anecdotes*. Berkeley, CA. Unpublished Manuscript, 1953. Sonoma County History and Genealogy Library.

Smith, Emma C. "Recollections of a Pioneer Mother." *Grizzly Bear*. Los Angeles & San Francisco, CA: Grizzly Bear Publishing Company, March-May 1923.

Introduction

[1] As it happened, the Carriger family was on the trail to California just a couple of weeks ahead of the Fowler family in 1846. Christian's son, Nicholas Carriger, kept a diary of their journey west from Missouri (Morgan, *Overland in 1846*, 143-158). Unfortunately, Christian Carriger died while crossing the Sierra Nevada Mountains at Lake Mary near Donner Summit on September 26, 1846. The author is related to Christian and Levisa Carriger through their older son John Thomas Carriger.

Chapter 1 - From the Old Country to a New Country

<u>Selected References</u>

Dunne, Amy Cresswell. *Lineage Book - National Society of the Daughters of the American Revolution. Volume 141, 1918.* Washington, D.C.: Daughters of the American Revolution, 1934.

[2] There is no record of when John Fowler arrived in the British Colonies. If he came as a child with his family, there would probably be a mention of them in the family stories. The lack of any such documentation and the commonness of young Scottish men immigrating to the colonies make it more likely John came as a young man.

[3] John Fowler was a private in the 12th Albany County Militia Regiment in Captain Aylsworth's company led by Colonel Van Schoonhoven.

[4] The German Lutheran Church of Johnstown was on the corner of Perry and Green Streets. Fowler Mallett wrote in his family history that the Fowler family engaged in farming, building, and law and that a brother of John Fowler Sr. built the first church with a steeple in Albany, something that other authors have sometimes wrongly attributed to John or his son William Fowler. If Peter Fowler was John's brother, it would explain Mallett's claim that a brother of John Fowler built the first church in Albany with a steeple. Albany had churches with steeples as early as 1715, so it is unlikely that a Fowler built the first one in town. However, if this family story has any merit, the location was probably somewhere nearby like the church Peter Fowler built in Johnstown, which had a steeple and was built around the right time. There is no record indicating William was involved in building this church. However, given his later works of this scale and that he was 36 years old at the time, it is possible.

[5] Fowler Mallett writes of William living in Rochester with a small family, then returning to Albany. Rochester in 1800 was still just forming and not a place for a young family, but if true, William may have gotten a taste for life on the frontier there. However, the family is not mentioned in the 1877 History of Monroe County. Also, Mallett seems unsure of the family connection to Rochester, which he speculated might be through William, John, or even another unknown sibling.

[6] There is no clear record of who Kitty's parents were or where her family was from. The only likely match found for Fowler Mallett's origin story was a family with three brothers named Speed in Columbia County, 35 miles from Albany. They were in the Dutch Reformed Church. The church affiliation seems to have been on their mother's side, and the mother's family was of German descent from New York, not Pennsylvania. The father was of English descent. In addition to these discrepancies, there are no records of a girl born to any of the Speed brothers around 1801 that could be Kitty. However, Dutch Reformed Church Membership Records as well as US and New York Census records for Claverack and Hillsdale in Columbia County show that one of the brothers, Henry Speed, was married to Elizabeth and they had children. While William and Kitty Fowler named their first boy and girl after themselves, their next boy and girl were named John Henry and Ann Eliza. Though not proof, it could be that John Henry and Ann Eliza were named after their grandparents: John Fowler and Henry Speed and Ann Keith Fowler and Elizabeth Mapes Speed. For another version of Kitty's childhood, some genealogists speculate that she was from the Speed families that moved from Virginia into Speedville, Tompkins County, New York. However, there are no records of children named Catherine born to them, nor are there records of them living in Albany, a considerable 150 miles away.

[7] The DAR records (Dunne, *Lineage Book*, 1918) show John and Elizabeth marrying in 1815. In the 1850 census, John is shown with his wife Elizabeth and their daughter Harriet Hopkins, who is by then 36. She is listed as born in New York, and given her age, she would have been born about 1814. Some genealogists list her birth date as April 1814.

[8] Alexander Fowler was born in June 1822 in Ohio.

Chapter 2 - A Growing Family Moves West

Selected References

Brink, McDonough & Company. *History of St. Clair County, Illinois: with illustrations descriptive of its scenery and biographical sketches of some of its prominent men and pioneers.* Philadelphia, PA: Brink, McDonough & Company, 1881.

National Historical Company. *The History of Henry and St. Clair Counties, Missouri, Containing a History of These Counties, Their Cities, Towns, etc., etc., Biographical Sketches of Their Citizens, General and Local Statistics, History of Missouri, Map of Henry and St. Clair Counties, etc.* St. Joseph, MO: National Historical Company, 1883.

[9] Various sources note either 1817 or 1818 as the year the Fowlers moved to the Illinois Territory.

[10] Some records have confused the mother Kitty (born Catherine Speed) with her daughter Catherine (born Catherine Fowler). It is understandable, since over time, they both had the last names Fowler and Musgrave, and their lives overlapped in several ways. Kitty's second husband, Calvin Musgrave, was close in age to Catherine. Also, Kitty and Catherine both lived in Hot Springs, California in the 1850s, and after Catherine's death in 1862, Kitty raised Catherine's children by Lewis Musgrave.

[11] *The History of Henry and St. Clair Counties* (National Historical Company, 1883, 978, 1044) mentions Fowler Bend and William Fowler living in Polk Township. The Cyrus and Owsley families are indicated as living in northern Polk Township, Missouri.

[12] Fowler Mallett wrote that the Fowler family in Albany had engaged in building and the practice of law, with sons being trained in one or the other. No records were found to back up this claim, and what is documented seems to contradict this. William Fowler's brother John was neither a builder nor a lawyer, and there is no record or indication that their father John Fowler pursued either profession. If indeed John Sr. had a brother Peter who was a builder, then one would expect John Sr. to have practiced law, which does not seem to be the case.

[13] John Hargrave's parents were Frederick and Susan Hargrave. John was likely born in Tennessee, or possibly Missouri. From 1819, John's father, Frederick, ran the ferry at Arrow Rock, Missouri, across the Missouri River and supplied traders on the Santa Fe Trail. Some time about 1838 or 1839, John's parents and his younger siblings moved to Van Buren, Arkansas.

[14] Calvin Musgrave was born to James Henry Musgrave and his wife, who was from Kentucky. John "The Quaker" Musgrave was born about 1668 in County Armagh, Ireland, to Oswin and Elizabeth Musgrave. John later married Mary Hastings.

Chapter 3 - On the Oregon Trail

Selected References

Bancroft, Hubert Howe. *The Works of Hubert Howe Bancroft. Volume XX. History of California. Vol. III. 1825-1840.* San Francisco: A. L. Bancroft & Company, 1885.

———. *The Works of Hubert Howe Bancroft. Volume XXI. History of California. Vol. IV. 1840-1845.* San Francisco, CA: A. L. Bancroft & Company, 1886.

Bidwell, John. "The First Emigrant Train to California." *Century Illustrated Monthly Magazine,* Volume 41, November 1890 to April 1891.

———. *A Journey To California With Observations About the Country, Climate and The Route to this Country.* San Francisco, CA: John Henry Nash Printer, 1937.

Brewer, Henry Bridgeman, and John M. Canse. *"Log of the Lausanne—V (Continued)." Oregon Historical Quarterly,* Vol. 30, No. 2, June 1929.

[15] Bidwell, *A Journey To California,* 1-2; Bidwell, "The First Emigrant Train," 120: note 1.

Bidwell lists the members of his company on page 1 of *A Journey to California,* and he misspells William Fowler's name as "William Towler." Bidwell does later spell it correctly in *The First Emigrant Train to California* printed in the California Historical Collection on page 120, note 1.

[16] Brewer, *"Log of the Lausanne—V,"* 112.

[17] The Kelsey family is listed as "Kelso" in the 1840 U.S. Census for Weaubleau Township, Rives County, Missouri.

[18] The Hargrave family may have had experience as millwrights, and some sources say they owned a grist mill near Van Buren, Arkansas, though it may have been at Arrow Rock in Missouri. William Hargrave was born in Missouri to John Hargrave and Hannah Harrison on March 8, 1818. John and Hannah were from Virginia, but they were married in Tennessee. About 1819, John Hargrave and his brother Frederick moved their families to Arrow Rock, Missouri. See note 13 on William's cousin John Hargrave.

[19] Fowler, *Raising Stock in Napa Valley,* 3-7; Guinn, *Coast Counties Volume 1,* 305-306.

In the 1886 version of this story told to Bancroft, Henry said they were repeatedly robbed and had to eventually threaten the Walla Wallas with guns to get them to stop. In a 1904 version told by Guinn, this event is framed as the party being surrounded and giving up many goods only to have them returned later by the chief.

[20] Not all parties arrived safely. The Applegates also traveled with the Gantt Party to Oregon that year. The large Applegate clan was another pioneer family from St. Clair County, Missouri, and they were likely known to the Fowlers. Nearing the end of their journey, three members of the Applegate group drowned in the Columbia River rapids when a boat capsized. The loss of the two nine-year-old Appleton boys and an old family friend prompted Jesse and Lindsay Applegate to help find a safer alternative route to Oregon in 1846. The Applegate Trail now carries their name.

[21] In June 1841, Isaiah Kelsey married Winifred Williams during the Bidwell-Bartleson Party's journey to Oregon. On July 30, 1841, Father DeSmet performed the marriage ceremony for Nancy Kelsey's sister Betsey and Richard Phelan. In May 1844, six months after Bill Fowler and Rebecca Kelsey's marriage, Rebecca's twin sister, Fanny, also married.

[22] The mill the Fowlers built may have been the "large Merchant Flouring Mill, belonging to Dr. McLaughin" mentioned by William Winter, who traveled with the Fowlers (Johnson and Winter, *Route Across the Rocky Mountains*, 43). It was one of the first flour mills in Oregon and was built at the time the Fowlers were there.

Chapter 4 - From Oregon to California

Selected References

Camp, Charles L., and James Clyman. *James Clyman, American Frontiersman 1792-1881: The Adventures Of A Trapper And Covered Wagon Emigrant As Told In His Own Reminiscences And Diaries.* San Francisco, CA: California Historical Society, 1928.

[23] Isaiah Kelsey and Loretta Kelsey stayed behind in Oregon with their families. Later their mother, Susan, would join them.

[24] Fowler, *Raising Stock in Napa Valley*, 10-12; Fowler, "Raise The Old Bear Flag"; Bancroft, *History of California Vol. IV,* 444-445, 453, 697-698; Johnson and Winter, *Route Across the Rocky Mountains*, 48-50, 73-77.

Johnson and Winter wrote that there were thirty-seven people in the Kelsey Party: thirteen women and children, and the rest were men from America, England, France, Mexico, and four Native

American tribes (Johnson and Winter, 73). Bancroft wrote that there were thirty-six people and listed twelve of the men, which he learned from letters between Sutter and Larkin (Bancroft, Vol. IV, 444). Henry Fowler wrote that they "had some Hudson Bay men for guides." This is the author's list of thirty-five people, accounting for all thirteen women and children. There is uncertainty about the identity of some of the men (marked by an *) since perhaps two or three other single men were in the group. The Kelsey Party included: David Kelsey, Susan Jane Kelsey (David's wife), Benjamin Kelsey (David's son), Nancy Kelsey (Benjamin's wife), Martha Kelsey (Benjamin's daughter), Margaret Kelsey (Benjamin's daughter), Samuel Kelsey (David's son), Lucretia Applegate Kelsey (Samuel's wife), William Kelsey (Samuel's son), Sarah Kelsey (Samuel's daughter), Joseph Kelsey (Samuel's son), Lucy Kelsey (Samuel's daughter), Andrew Kelsey (David's son), Rebecca Kelsey Fowler (David's daughter and Bill's wife), Bill Fowler (William's son and husband of Rebecca), Francis "Fanny" Kelsey Buzzell (Buzzell's wife and David Kelsey's daughter), Joseph Willard Buzzell (Fanny's husband), America Kelsey (David's daughter), Davy Crockett Kelsey (David's son), William Fowler Sr. (Bill's father), Henry Fowler (Bill's brother), William Hargrave, Granville P. Swift, William Winter, *Overton Johnson, William Bennett, David T. Bird, Petitoo (Spanish-Native American #1), Iroquois Native American man #2 (*Ignace?), French-Native American man #3, Native American man #4, Hudson Bay man #1 (*Michel Laframboise as guide?), Hudson Bay man #2 (*Baptiste Moliere as guide?), *Hudson Bay man #3 (British?), *Joel P. Walker (had gone to Oregon with Ben Kelsey).

[25] Camp and Clyman, *James Clyman, American Frontiersman*, 153-154.
        This advice was for a party traveling the Siskiyou Trail in 1845.
[26] Johnson and Winter, *Route Across the Rocky Mountains*, 73-74.
[27] Fowler, "Raise The Old Bear Flag."

Chapter 5 - Arriving in Alta California

Selected References

Larkin, Thomas O. *Correspondence with Bill and Rebecca Fowler December 1844 to March 1845.* Unpublished Letters. Thomas O. Larkin papers collection. Originals at The Bancroft Library, University of California, Berkeley. BANC MSS C-B 37-45.

Wilkes, Charles. *Narrative of the United States Exploring Expedition. During the years 1838, 1839, 1840, 1841, 1842.* Philadelphia, PA: Lea and Blanchard, 1845.

[28] Larkin, *Correspondence with Bill and Rebecca Fowler*; Weber, Lin. *Old Napa Valley: The History to 1900.* St. Helena, CA: Wine Ventures Publishing, 1998. 62-63.

[29] Larkin. *Correspondence with Bill and Rebecca Fowler.*

[30] Rebecca married Grove C. Cook in December 1845 at Sutter's Fort and subsequently married Dr. Christopher Grattan about 1853.

[31] R. H. Dana's *Two Years Before the Mast* is an interesting account of the hide and tallow trade from the perspective of a sailor collecting and transporting these goods.

[32] Duflot de Mofras, *Exploration du territoire de l'Orégon,* 1844. as quoted in Bancroft, *History of California Vol. IV,* 260.

[33] Wilkes, *United States Exploring Expedition,* 196-197.

Chapter 6 - Putting Down Roots in the Napa Valley

Selected References

Palmer, Lyman L., W. F. Wallace, Harry Laurenz Wells, and Tillie Kanaga. *History of Napa and Lake Counties, California: comprising their geography ... together with a full and particular record ... also separate histories ....* San Francisco, CA: Slocum, Bowen, 1881.

Wright, Elizabeth Cyrus. *The Early Upper Napa Valley.* Calistoga, CA: Sharpsteen Museum Reprints, 1991. Copy of original manuscript at Bancroft Library, BANC MSS 73/122 c. Many reprinted versions exist at various historical libraries in California.

[34] James Clyman noted that the Kelseys and William Hargrave hunted in the valley in 1845. According to William Hargrave (Hargrave and Petroff, *California in 1846*), he hunted and trapped for a living for a few years after arriving in California.

[35] George Yount was born in 1794, which would have made him about 51 years old in 1845.

[36] Over the years, the Kelseys and other families lived in the cabin started by the Fowlers, and it is currently remembered as the "Kelsey House site." The site is near the intersection of Diamond Mountain Road and Highway 29.

Chapter 7 - The Battle for California and the Bear Flag Revolt

<u>Selected References</u>

Bancroft, Hubert Howe. *The Works of Hubert Howe Bancroft. Volume XXII. History of California. Vol. V. 1846-1848.* San Francisco: The History Company, 1886.

Hargrave, William H., and Ivan Petroff. *California in 1846.* Interviews of William Hargrave by Ivan Petroff for the Bancroft Library. 1878. Original at Bancroft Library. BANC MSS C-D 97.

Warner, Barbara R. *The Men of the Bear Flag Revolt and Their Heritage.* Norman, OK: Arthur H. Clark, 1996.

[37] Fowler, *Raising Stock in Napa Valley*, 22-23.

[38] Henry Fowler (Fowler, *Raising Stock in Napa Valley*, 24) said in his 1886 interview with Bancroft that he was at Yount's during the taking of Sonoma, making it sound like he was not at the Bale Mill gathering. Henry's grandson, Fowler Mallett (Mallett, *Genealogical Notes and Anecdotes*, 89), recounted that Henry and William were at the Bale Mill gathering and that they argued for less violent action.

[39] Stories vary widely as to who made the first flag. The author presents here his best account of what seems to be true given all available sources.

[40] So many women were given credit for donating their bloomers that it is hard to say from exactly whose skirts the flag was born, though Nancy Kelsey does seem a very likely candidate.

[41] Due to conflicting accounts, which flag flew and when may never be known. However, many sources testified to Peter Storm's flag being made on June 13.

Chapter 8 - The Family Follows on the California Trail

<u>Selected References</u>

Allen, William W., and Richard B. Avery. *California Gold Book, First Nugget: Its Discovery and Discoverers and Some of the Results Proceeding Therefrom.* San Francisco, CA: Donohue & Henneberry, 1893.

Howell, Elizabeth Owsley. *Owsley Genealogy: Calistoga Pioneers—Napa County.* Transcribed Letter. Undated. Manuscript MS-45. Napa County Historical Society.

Morgan, Dale. *Overland in 1846: Diaries and Letters of the California-Oregon Trail, Vol. I & II*. Lincoln, NE: University of Nebraska Press, 1993.

Niles, Hezekiah et al. *Niles' National Register, Contains Political, Historical, Geographical ... Documents, Essays and Facts: Together with Notices ... and Record of the Events of the Times. ... Volume 71*. Baltimore, MD: Jeremiah Hughs, Editor, 1847.

[42] Johnson and Winter, *Route Across the Rocky Mountains*, 129-130.

[43] Johnson and Winter, *Route Across the Rocky Mountains*, 122-129, 130-134.

[44] "The Independence *Expositor* recommends ...." *Missouri Reporter* (St. Louis, MO), March 9, 1846, as quoted in Morgan, *Overland in 1846* Vol. 2, 485.

[45] Elizabeth Owsley Howell (Howell, *Owsley Genealogy*) does not list Bill Fowler among the group, despite his other family members being listed. This may be because Bill did not set out when her group started, and instead, met up with them in Independence. The most likely reason for this is that Bill may have headed to Independence earlier to be hired as a guide.

[46] Harlan, California '46 to '88, 36.

[47] Allen and Avery, *California Gold Book*, 64.

[48] Niles et al, *Niles' National Register*, 151.

Chapter 9 - A Perilous Passage

Selected References

Bryant, Edwin. *What I Saw in California*. New York, NY: D. Appleton & Co, 1848.

Hastings, Lansford W. *The Emigrants' Guide to Oregon and California*. Cincinnati, OH: George Conclin, 1845.

Korns, J. Roderic. *West from Fort Bridger: The Pioneering of the Immigrant Trails Across Utah, 1846-1850*. Salt Lake City, UT: Utah State Historical Society, 1951. Also published in *Utah Historical Quarterly*, Volume 19, No. 1/4, January, April, July, October 1951.

Murphy, Virginia Reed. "Across the Plains in the Donner Party: A Personal Narrative of the Overland Trip to California." *Century Illustrated Monthly Magazine*. Volume 42. May 1891 to October 1891. New York, NY: Scribner & Company. The Century Company, 1891.

⁴⁹ Hastings, *Emigrants' Guide to Oregon and California*, 137-138.

⁵⁰ Heinrich Lienhard traveled in the Hoppe Party, which caught up with the Harlan Party in Weber Canyon. The number of wagons in the Harlan Party varies by account, but many sources cite about sixty.

⁵¹ This group is known as the Bryant-Russell Party. It included diarist Edwin Bryant and previous party leader William Russell.

⁵² James Mather and two others traveling with him caught up with the Harlan Party on July 25.

⁵³ James Hudspeth's group on horseback traveled faster than those with wagons, though they had trouble finding their way through the Wasatch Range. Hudspeth explored the nearby canyons looking for a better trail suitable for wagons, while most of his party deemed the rough terrain impassable for them. Having scouted the area, Hudspeth left his party to go back to check on the progress of Hastings and the Harlan-Young Party. Meanwhile, Hastings went back and found the Hoppe Party, which he then led along the route the Harlan-Young Party had used.

⁵⁴ Allen and Avery, *California Gold Book*, 63-64.

⁵⁵ Jacob Harlan's account puts the wedding between Fort Bridger and The Salt Lake Desert when Bill Fowler lost his oxen (Harlan, *California '46 to '88*, 44). Jennie Wimmer described a celebration upon reaching the Great Salt Lake while camped near the Jordan River and present-day Salt Lake City (Allen and Avery, *California Gold Book*, 63-64). It seems likely that these were the same event. Korns puts the Harlan Party's crossing of the Jordan River at the ford at North Temple.

⁵⁶ Korns, *West from Fort Bridger*, 189, 207-208.

⁵⁷ Bryant, *What I Saw in California*, 170; Korns, *West from Fort Bridger*, 83.

⁵⁸ Murphy, "Across the Plains in the Donner Party," 416.

⁵⁹ Nicholas Carriger's diary (Morgan, *Overland in 1846*, 143-158) has his party at the Greenwood Cutoff on July 18, ten days behind the Harlan Party, who would have passed that spot on July 8 in order to arrive at Fort Bridger on July 16. The Carrigers reached the spot where Hastings Cutoff rejoined the main trail near present-day Elko, Nevada on August 22. It took them 45 days following the main trail. Similarly, according to William E. Taylor's diary, the main route took him 47 days (Morgan, *Overland in 1846*, 126-128). The Harlans were recuperating after the Great Salt Desert crossing, continuing on August 24 for the 14-day journey to Mary's River around the Ruby Mountains, which would have them

arriving about September 7. Therefore the Harlans spent 53 days on the Hastings Cutoff. In Heinrich Lienhard's diary, he wrote that they arrived at Mary's River on September 7 and met a small company that had left Fort Bridger twelve or thirteen days after they did and traveled along the main route. It seems the Hastings Cutoff took about a week or two longer than the main trail. The Donner Party did not reach Mary's River for another 19 days. In all, the Hastings Cutoff from Fort Bridger to Mary's River was about 390 miles, whereas the corresponding section of the main trail was about 460 miles. The cutoff certainly was not the hundreds of miles shorter Hastings had promised, nor was it a time saver. It was also much more dangerous.

[60] William McCutchen and Charles Stanton were sent ahead for supplies. McCutchen stayed at Fort Sutter, too ill to travel back, which saved his life. His wife survived the ordeal, but their daughter did not. Stanton returned to the Donner Party with mules, food, and two Indian guides. All three died. Luis and Salvador, the Native American men who were sent with Charles, were shot and eaten by members of the Donner Party.

[61] The Harlan and Boggs Parties most likely used the newly discovered Roller Pass, which was somewhat easier than Donner Pass. It was so named for the technique of using a log across the top of the pass as a roller for the cable that was attached to the wagons on one side and the oxen on the other. By driving the oxen down the far side of the pass, they pulled the wagons up. Roller Pass is described in Nicholas Carriger's diary (Morgan, *Overland in 1846*, 143-158) and was possibly found by their party when they crossed the Sierra at the end of September, just weeks before the Harlan Party passed through.

Chapter 10 - Buildings and Wedding Bells

<u>Selected References</u>
"Pioneer of '46 Writes of the Petaluma Adobe: Reminiscence of the Late General Vallejo." *Press Democrat* (Santa Rosa, CA), January 21, 1910. 2:1.

Vallejo, Mariano Guadalupe. *Private Letter to Miss N. L. Denman*. Photocopied Letter, May 16, 1889.

[62] Vallejo, *Private Letter to Miss N. L. Denman.*

[63] "Pioneer of '46," *Press Democrat.*

       William Boggs was 20 years old at the time he stayed in the Petaluma Adobe during the winter of 1846-47.

[64] "Pioneer of '46," *Press Democrat.*

[65] Harlan, *California '46 to '88*, 108, 115-117.

[66] Harlan, *California '46 to '88*, 117-119.

[67] Smith, "Recollections of a Pioneer Mother," April 1923, 4.

[68] William Leidesdorff also owned the first cargo warehouse in San Francisco.

Chapter 11 - Gold Transforms California

<u>Selected References</u>

Bancroft, Hubert Howe. *The Works of Hubert Howe Bancroft. Volume XIX. History of California. Vol. II. 1801-1824.* San Francisco: A. L. Bancroft & Company, 1885.

"California." *Polynesian* (Honolulu, HI), Volume 5, Number 9, July 15, 1848. 34-35.

Domogalla, Kent. *Looking for the Past in Calistoga: A Historical Timeline and a Street and Pictorial Guide to Selected Historic Properties and Locations.* Calistoga, CA: Sharpsteen Museum Association, 1998.

"E. T. Bale and Wife Deeds." Napa County Records, Book "A," 80-81. Digital scan of handwritten deed by Napa County Recorder, accessed March 30, 2020.

Skjeie, Sheilla. *Edward Turner Bale: A Pioneer Miller in the Napa Valley.* California Department of Parks and Recreation, August 19, 1976. Manuscript in collection of Napa Historical Society. MS-90.

[69] Smith, "Recollections of a Pioneer Mother," March 1923, 29.

       Clark's Point was at about the intersection of Broadway and Front Streets. The Yerba Buena cove had been mostly filled in by 1853. What is now the Embarcadero area was originally a cove that ran from Clark's Point to Rincon Point at Spear and Harrison Streets and came in as far as Montgomery and First Streets. Portsmouth Square was a natural spot for a plaza as it was a high point in the middle of the shoreline of the cove.

[70] The date of the discovery of gold is usually stated as January 24, 1848. Allen and Avery (Allen and Avery, *California Gold Book*, 5-7) claim the date was January 19, 1848, and they give their proof.

[71] "California," *Polynesian.*

[72] Fowler, *Raising Stock in Napa Valley,* 14-16.

[73] The Hastings Cutoff guide, James Hudspeth, accompanied the Fowlers and Hargrave to the Gold Country in 1849. The cousin that Henry Fowler went to Placerville with in 1850 was also named Henry Fowler and was the son of John Fowler Jr., William's brother from Albany.

     John and his family moved from Ohio to St. Joseph, Indiana, in 1832, and in 1835, John was issued a license for a tavern there. After the Gold Rush, John Fowler Jr. traveled back and forth from Indiana to California, living in Napa Valley at times. He was known by William Fowler's children as "Uncle Johnny." Some of John and Elizabeth's children moved to California as well. Their son Henry, who went gold mining in Placerville with his cousin Henry Fowler, lived in California near the Fowlers in Napa Valley in 1860. John Fowler Jr. died in 1860, just after returning from California to South Bend, Indiana.

     Find A Grave, https://www.findagrave.com/memorial/162821197, accessed July 3, 2020, has the following note: "Family speculation is that, after Harriet Fowler was born 1814 in New York, the family moved to Licking County, Ohio. After Henry Clay was born in 1834, the Fowler family moved to St. Joseph County, Indiana. John F. Fowler Jr. traveled back and forth to California [Napa County] from Indiana [South Bend] occasionally. He had been living in California with his wife Elizabeth Howey for some years before returning to South Bend, Indiana where he died in the home of his son, Alexander Fowler" ... "St. Joseph Valley Register, December 6, 1860: 'In South Bend, November 30th, at the residence of his son, Alexander Fowler. JOHN FOWLER, Senior, late from California, in the 79th year of his age: [inscription] "He has made his last journey to mingle his dust With the loved ones his hearthstone had blessed; And calm and content with this hope and this trust, He laid him down sweetly to rest."'"

[74] "E. T. Bale and Wife Deeds," Napa County Records.

     The low sale price may indicate that the sale was made as payment for carpentry work done by the Fowlers. In terms of the timing of the sale, documents offer contradicting information. Some sources list the date of this sale as April 1849. However, the deed was filed a year and four months later on August 2, 1850. It was dated 1850 in three places, signed by Bale, and witnessed by Hiram

Smith and Henry Owsley. On the other hand, Bale's gravestone and other sources list his date of death as October 9, 1849, after the April 1849 sale, but well before the 1850 recording. Reflecting this confusion, historian Hubert Bancroft wrote that Bale died in 1849 or 1850. Therefore, the exact date of these sales remains unresolved.

[75] When Jacob Harlan sold the dairy, Charles Gough returned to Baltimore to bring his twin brother to San Francisco. Gough had told Jacob Harlan that the twins were so identical their father could not tell them apart. This is echoed in a July 27, 1895 article in the *San Francisco Call.* Gough and his twin brother were both volunteer fire-fighters, along with yet another Gough brother.

[76] The 1850 U.S. Census for Napa Valley, CA was dated twelve days before young George Harlan III was born, and therefore he is not listed.

[77] Young George Harlan III would also meet an untimely end and die at the young age of 23 when he was run over by a logging truck.

Chapter 12 - Ranching at Hot Springs and Venturing to Hawaii

[78] "Passengers," *Polynesian* (Honolulu, HI), March 2, 1850. 3:2.

[79] "Passengers," *Polynesian* (Honolulu, HI), June 11, 1853. 3:1.

Chapter 13 - Shifting Fortunes

Selected References

Draper, Elias Johnson. *An Autobiography of Elias Johnson Draper, a Pioneer of California. Containing Some Thrilling Incidents Relative to Crossing the Plains by Ox Team, and Some Very Interesting Particulars of Life in California in the Early Days [1853].* Fresno, CA: Evening Democrat Print, 1904.

Napa Valley Genealogical and Biographical Society. "Napa County, California, Marriages 1850-1905." Book A, Page 19. Manuscript, 1996.

[80] "Correspondence of the Alta California." *Daily Alta California* (San Francisco, CA), Volume 1, Number 61, March 11, 1850. 2:3.

[81] In 1860 Edmundson was the Sheriff of Brooklyn, now a southern part of the city of Oakland, California, where he lived with Malinda and their growing family. They later moved to Idaho City, Idaho, where

Edmundson practiced law for several years. Malinda Harlan Fowler Edmundson died in September 1876.

[82] The 1858 Harlan home was still at 19251 San Ramon Valley Boulevard south of the town of San Ramon as of November 2020.

[83] Elijah Harlan's farm was in Kosciusko County, Indiana.

[84] Harlan, *California '46 to '88*, 198-208.

[85] Wright, *Early Upper Napa Valley*, 24.

[86] "State Correspondence." *Daily Alta California* (San Francisco, CA), Volume 18, No. 6015, August 30, 1866. 1:5.

[87] James Musgrave, 26 years old, married Nancy Philpot on April 13, 1868. Together they had a baby girl named Lillian Bell Musgrave, though it seems the couple did not stay together long. In the 1880 census, James is listed as working in a saloon in Sonoma and married, though he and his wife continued to live apart. In the same census, his wife, Nancy Philpott Musgrave, is shown to be still living in Mendocino County and is also listed as married. In the 1900 and 1910 censuses, Nancy is listed as a widow living in Mendocino County, but in 1920, she is listed as divorced. James and Nancy may have gotten divorced at some point, but it is not known for certain or when it may have happened. In April of 1881, the *Daily Republican* of Santa Rosa reported that James was in the hospital and his half-sister Minerva was looking after him. The next day, the same paper reported that he had died on April 6, 1881. James was 39 years old and was survived by Nancy and their young daughter, Lillian Bell Musgrave. Nancy Philpott Musgrave outlived James Musgrave by forty-four years, and she even outlived their daughter by a few years. She died at the home of her granddaughter in Petaluma on October 10, 1925, at the age of 67.

[88] Alfred was seen as the black sheep of the family, at least according to Fowler Mallett. Over the course of twenty years, he had three wives with whom he had five children. Alfred spent time with members of the Kelsey family and got into trouble joining them in their malicious treatment of Native Americans. The 1880 census lists Alfred's residence as the prison in Tulare, California, where he was serving time for a felony. Bennett Musgrave, an uncle of Calvin and Alfred, lived with his son Thomas near the Fowlers and Musgraves in Hot Springs in 1850. In 1864 Bennett Musgrave died near Panama on a trip back to California.

[89] The Magness family lived in Arkansas briefly before continuing to Texas, where Catherine was born. While the family story was that Henry

Fowler met Catherine Magness in Texas when she was a baby, the dates don't fit together. Henry mentions the family staying briefly in Arkansas (Fowler, *Raising Stock*), but she wasn't born there. There is no evidence of Henry being in Texas between 1841 and 1843, or in 1845, as Mallett wrote. Mallett describes Henry Fowler leaving mid-summer of 1845 and riding on horseback to Mexico City to validate and record the title of their land purchased from Dr. Bale. He then, supposedly, circled through Arkansas and Texas on his way back, meeting the Magness family in Austin, Texas. Such a journey would have taken about a year and could not have been done on horseback without many pack animals to carry supplies. Most would have taken a ship to the coast of Mexico and ride from there. Additionally, Henry was back in Napa Valley in June of 1846. It seems fair to assume that the story is not true. Another explanation is that William Hargrave met the Magness family while visiting his uncle in Van Buren, Arkansas, and he later recognized them in San Francisco.

[90] William Hargrave and Anna Collins were married by Baptist minister Stephen Riley. It was William's second marriage. William Hargrave was married in Missouri before traveling west with the Fowlers. He married Margaret Anderson on August 20, 1836, in Henry County, Missouri. William and Margaret were living together in Jackson, Livingston County, in 1840. There is no further record of Margaret, so she may have died. William Hargrave's brother James married Martha Anderson on March 7, 1839. Martha was likely related to Margaret.

[91] Catherine Fowler's first husband, John Hargrave, and William Hargrave were first cousins. Their fathers, Frederick and John Hargrave, respectively, were brothers. The brothers moved from Tennessee with their families to Arrow Rock, Missouri, in 1819.

Chapter 14 - The Wild West and Lewis Musgrave

Selected References

Cook, David J., and Cook, John W. *Hands Up: or Thirty-Five Years of Detective Life in the Mountains and on the Plains*. Denver, CO: W. F. Robinson Printing Company, 1897.

"The Garroters." *Rocky Mountain News* (Denver, CO), November 23, 1868. 1:2.

"The Hanging of Musgrove." *Cheyenne Leader* (Cheyenne, WY), No. 58, November 25, 1868. 1:4.

"The Hanging of Musgrove." *Rocky Mountain News* (Denver, CO), November 24, 1868. 1:3.

"How Ab. Loomis Lost a Mule." *Fort Collins Courier*, January 20, 1887. 7:5.

"Town & County Notices." *The Weekly Calistogian* (Calistoga, CA), May 24, 1876. 3:1.

Watrous, Ansel. *History of Larimer County, Colorado*. Fort Collins, CO: The Courier Printing & Publishing Company, 1911.

[92] "How Ab. Loomis Lost a Mule," *Fort Collins Courier*.

[93] "An Old-Time Desperado." *Leadville Daily Herald* (Leadville, CO), April 14, 1885. 4:3.

[94] Cook and Cook, *Hands Up*, 93-94.

[95] Cook and Cook, *Hands Up*, 100-111.

[96] The Hanging of Musgrove," *Cheyenne Leader*.

The two letters Musgrave wrote on the bridge help to confirm that L. H. Musgrove is indeed the same man as Lewis H. Musgrave of the Fowler family. There is the similarity of the names, the difference being a common variation in the spelling of the last name. The letter addressed to his brother mentions the need to care for his children in Napa Valley, which is consistent with the death of Lewis' wife Catherine and his abandonment of the children who were living with their grandmother Kitty in Hot Springs. The brother he is writing to is W. C. Musgrove, which corresponds with Lewis' older brother William who lived in or near Como Depot in Panola County, Mississippi during the last half of the 1800s. The other letter is addressed to his wife, Mary Musgrove, 22 years old and living alone in Cheyenne, Wyoming, in the 1870 census. Given the death of his first wife, it is not unreasonable to believe that Lewis remarried a young woman in Wyoming. This also fits with Fowler Mallett's version of the story in which he says Lewis remarried and had two children, even though there are no records of the children. Fowler Mallett also has a version of this story indicating it is quite likely that the family claimed Lewis as family, although in Mallett's version he kindly believes Lewis' letters at face value and claims his innocence.

There is another version of how Lewis Musgrave was captured, but given how it contradicts the stories in newspapers of the time, it is probably not true, That version claims that Abner Loomis, a farmer and vegetable seller near Laporte, tricked Musgrave into coming to his ranch by saying that he had a valuable horse that Lewis had lost. Lawmen were lying in wait and captured Musgrave. By all contemporary accounts, Musgrave was captured in Wyoming, not Colorado, as Loomis claimed. David J. Cook tells a more accurate and fairly complete version of the Musgrove story in his 1897 reminiscence as a lawman, titled *Hands Up: or Thirty-Five Years of Detective Life in the Mountains and on the Plains.*

[97] "The Hanging of Musgrove," *Cheyenne Leader.*

[98] Cook and Cook, *Hands Up*, 117-118.

[99] "L. H. Musgrove" was the last episode of *Stories of the Century,* an Emmy award-winning series. It aired March 11, 1955, with John Archer playing L. H. Musgrove.

Chapter 15 - The End of One Era and the Start of Another

Selected References
Adams, I. C. *Memoirs & Anecdotes of Early Days in Calistoga.* Calistoga, CA: Sharpsteen Museum Association, 1946 (reprinted).

Archuleta, Kay. *The Brannan Saga: Early Calistoga.* Calistoga, CA: Illuminations Press, 1991.

"Death of a Pioneer." *Daily Alta California* (San Francisco, CA), Volume 17, Number 5453, February 9, 1865. 1:2.

[100] Martha Ritchie was the widow of Archibald Ritchie, who had died nine months earlier.

[101] "Death of a Pioneer," *Daily Alta California.*

[102] The East Napa Land Company partners were Henry Fowler, C. B. Hartson, Cayetano Juarez, Judge Burnett, and Peter D. Bailey.

Chapter 16 - The Passing of the Last Pioneers

Selected References
"Another Pioneer Gone." *Napa Daily Journal,* September 23, 1890. 3:2.

Boggs, William M. *Late Henry Fowler, Father of Napa, Cal., Pioneers of 1843 & 4.* Letter to J. L. Gillis, California State Librarian, July 24, 1906. Original and transcript at California Library History Room, Sacramento, CA.

"Henry Fowler, Early Settler of Napa, Dead." *San Francisco Chronicle*, October 19, 1904. 3.

Morris, Charles. *The San Francisco Calamity by Earthquake and Fire: A Complete and Accurate Account of the Fearful Disaster ....* New York, NY: W. E. Scull, 1906.

Munro-Fraser, J. P. *History of Contra Costa County, California: Including Its Geography ... Together With a Record ... Also, Incidents of Pioneer Life; And Biographical Sketches ....* Volumes 1 & 2. San Francisco, CA: W. A. Slocum & Company, 1882.

"A Pioneer Citizen Gone." *Contra Costa Gazette* (Martinez, CA), April 3, 1875. 3:1.

[103] Henry and Catherine Fowler's only son, Albert, died of pneumonia on December 4, 1871, at the young age of 6. His death was felt deeply by the family and continued to be a source of sadness for his parents for the rest of their lives.

[104] "A Pioneer Citizen Gone," *Contra Costa Gazette*; Munro-Fraser, *Contra Costa County Including Its Geography*, 574.

[105] William Henry Fowler III was alternately listed as divorced and widowed in the census records for Happy Camp, CA. It seems he married Wilhelmina Belle Keffer (Fowler, Jensen, Ince) (1878-1961) about 1893 and probably in Siskiyou County, CA while living in Oak Bar, CA. They were divorced by 1897. They had two children together, John Harlan Fowler (1894-1979) and Inez May Fowler (Jones, Brown, Wilson) (1896-1977).

[106] The Palace Hotel was sold to George C. Tryon in 1900.

[107] In December of 1873, Anna Collins Hargrave, William Hargrave's wife, passed away. She was just 35 years old. Together, Anna and William had seven children, and all but one survived their mother, though another would die a month after Anna's death. William was 55 years old and continued to live with his children on Calistoga Street in Napa near Henry Fowler's home until his death.

[108] During this time, Henry and Catherine had a home in San Francisco at 1313 Jones Street between Clay and Washington Streets.

[109] "Henry Fowler, Early Settler of Napa, Dead," *San Francisco Chronicle*.

[110] Boggs, "*Late Henry Fowler.*"

[111] Catherine Magness Fowler survived her husband, Henry, by thirteen years. She died at age 75 on October 25, 1917, in Berkeley. She stayed in the Napa home until 1909 and then lived with her daughters. All four of her daughters survived her.

[112] Morris, *The San Francisco Calamity*, 50.

Index

Acknowledgments

I'd like to thank the many people who have contributed in large and small ways to the making of this book. The number and quality of resources available online these days are astonishing and wonderful, and I am grateful to those who make it so. The reference librarians at local history libraries are a public treasure. Sheli Smith of the Napa County Historical Society, Katherine Rinehart, Sherry Eiselen, Maggie Hohle, and Steve Harrison were particularly helpful. The biggest thanks go to my wife, Beth Meredith, for her constructive, insightful, creative, and patient help all along the way.

About the Author

Eric Storm is a 7th generation Californian and the 4th great-grandson of William Fowler. By nature, Eric is a researcher, designer, educator, and connector of dots, and he has spent hundreds of hours digging into his family tree to unearth the details of their stories. He and his wife live in Sonoma County and happen to be just twenty-four miles from the old Fowler Ranch in Calistoga.

www.ingramcontent.com/pod-product-compliance
Lightning Source LLC
Chambersburg PA
CBHW071438090426
42737CB00011B/1704